PRAISE FOR

GROWING YOUR FAMILY:
Learn How to Flourish and Thrive as a Military Family

"The wonder that is the military spouse/family was a part of my life for over thirty years. As a former military child care professional, I worked with them both in the States and overseas. In *Growing Your Family*, Mrs. Alimo has captured the essence of military family life by sharing her personal life and professional knowledge in a warm, practical way that all military parents can easily relate to within their own family structure. I have read many books and articles about military children and families, but this one touches on the real struggles of everyday military life and offers practical and doable solutions. I would have appreciated a book like this during my working years, and I see it becoming a go-to resource book for a wide variety of professionals (trainers, public school teachers, community outreach, etc.) that want to better understand the military lifestyle!"

**—Laura Knutson, Retired Military Child Care
Professional, Former Military Spouse, Mom**

"Pearl's wisdom, kind spirit, and strong support of the military life shines bright in her new book, *Growing Your Family: Learn How to Flourish and Thrive as a Military Family*. Her experiences from child rearing to family balance, whether during deployment or while on base, help her reader understand it is possible and much needed to create a life of normalcy while supporting the military. Ease any fears you may have of a military lifestyle by reading Pearl's reality and pondering the reflective questions at the end of each chapter. This will leave you feeling her support and friendship through each curve life throws as you walk the path she has cleared for you."

—**Carrie Scarborough Kinnard, Author of** *From the Grit Comes a Pearl*

"You truly feel the passion, emotions, and strength in *Growing Your Family*. As a former military spouse, I find these situations so relevant to what we experience day to day—often questioning what I am doing, how I can handle this, and most importantly how I grow my family. The raw truth of growing your family while supporting your service member's commitment to this country is laid out beautifully in this book."

—**Diana Jimenez, Former Military Spouse, Mom**

"*Growing Your Family: Learn How to Flourish and Thrive as a Military Family* is the right book for the right time. It is skillfully written from start to finish, with great takeaways for both military families and non-military families. It is not a book that you read once and put aside. You can open any random page at any time and find something to catch your mind and heart. The book is practical, insightful and easy to read. Page after page, Mrs. Pearl Alimo masterfully captivates her readers and find ways to connect with them. As a wife, a mother, and a lawyer, I highly recommend *Growing Your Family: Learn How to Flourish and Thrive as a Military Family* to any book lover."

—**Nida Massala, Attorney, Educamatch Inc.**

"Pearl Alimo takes readers on a comprehensive journey into the daily challenges and joys of military family life. Her book, *Growing Your Family*, is a delightful guide full of important information for those of us who want to learn little tricks on how to deal with everything from deployment to parenting and enjoy life to its best along the way. I absolutely love the enormous number of resources she provides. The end-of-chapter reflective questions helped me organize my thoughts and reflect upon my own family dynamic. They are practical and will be an awesome addition to guide group discussions and book clubs."

—**Flávia Valdez, Military Spouse, Mom**

"I love this book! Pearl Alimo draws you in and shares her and her family's experiences in living color. The book is full of life, represented in advice, suggestions and resources for any family, and my favorite part is the interactive piece. She guides the reader in self-reflection questions that help the reader plan, prepare and apply pieces of the book to their own life. A beautiful read, from a beautiful human. I am blessed to call Pearl Alimo my friend."

—**April Hallback, Veteran, Surviving Military Spouse**

"*Growing Your Family* is an excellent resource on parenting with illustrations from real, natural, authentic stories of military families. It grew out of the author's vision of 'creating a home where we all can flourish—myself, my husband, our children. I also want anyone who enters our home, to feel the love of Christ and smell the sweet aroma of love, joy, kindness, hope, and peace.' Its focus is on how we can give comprehensive love to our children. . . . Indeed, this book makes fulfilling reading. It pulsates with rich content and real stories which effectively communicate great principles and practices of parenting. You will even read about a personal 'survival kit' in the bathroom! "Pearl Gifty Alimo, was raised by a single parent. So, it was not to her a completely strange experience to stay back and raise her children all alone, when her husband was deployed to defend and protect their country. But careful parental formation is needed to navigate this turf and to flourish and thrive as a military family. . . . I highly recommend this book."

—Jude Hama, President, Africa Bible Center for Disciple-Making (ABCD); Former CEO, Scripture Union; National Executive Director, Billy Graham Evangelistic Association Crusade in Ghana

"I have been a military spouse for over sixteen years. Sometimes we are referred to as seasoned military spouses, but I can tell you that just as Pearl said, it does not get easier. The years come with different challenges, and I enjoyed reading the different ideas for staying connected. As my child is nearing his teen years, I want to make sure that we communicate his dreams and goals and spend time talking about anything and everything. I want him to know that although this lifestyle can be challenging, we are here to support him. Being a teacher to military-connected children, I am also aware of the challenges they face as I see the struggles with my own child. I want them to know that I am there to listen and show empathy. We talk about the fun times and memories and countdown to the homecomings. Thank you for pouring your heart and soul into this book."

—April Romero, Military Spouse, Mother, Teacher

"Pearl G. Alimo takes you on a tour of her own life, revealing how to fully and joyously live your life in any circumstance being yourself, a wife, a mother, a career woman and a God lover. I highly recommend this book to anyone who truly wants to see ceaseless value being created right from their home eternally."

—Doreen Afesi-Kutsenejie, Wife, Mom, Banker (Ghana)

"What is a perfectly accurate description of life in a low-income neighborhood in Accra, Ghana, may seem a bit unreal or even shocking to many readers. *Growing Your Family* is an introspective journey about achieving your dreams irrespective of the humble beginnings that nurtured these dreams. Gifty Alimo's remarkable odyssey across three continents, captured so beautifully in this book, is a lesson in appreciating every little experience life throws at us and making the most of them."

—Samuel Bartels, Lawyer, Journalist, and Lecturer (Ghana)

DEDICATION

THIS BOOK IS DEDICATED to my fellow military spouses and moms who must stay behind to raise children with parents in uniform.

Also, for the parent in uniform who must say countless tearful goodbyes to your family because you must deploy to defend and protect our country.

Most importantly, to all military children, including my own. You are the inspiration behind this book. I salute you.

And finally, to my friend and husband Maxwell. Thank you for giving me a chance to grow our family with you and especially for making this dream a reality.

TABLE OF CONTENTS

FOREWORD

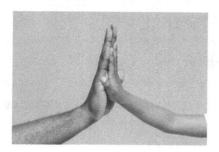

PERHAPS YOU ARE THE ACTIVE DUTY service member with a child and who has to say countless tearful goodbyes as you leave on yet another long deployment. You may be the military spouse who said *I do* and decided to start a family, not realizing exactly what it would mean to be the parent raising your children alone while the other parent was out there defending and protecting our country.

The struggle was real. The fears are there. Change comes all the time. Moves are a must, but victory is yours if you follow me through this book. We do it every day and sometimes you get used to the saying *I don't know how; I just do it.*

If there is something that I have learned most as a military spouse and mother raising three children is how to create a home from an empty space or to make something out of nothing. My goal is to share the raw truth of my experience raising our children as a Christian, an immigrant with a different upbringing and cultural background, and a military spouse who is pursuing a career of her own. I wouldn't say I know it all and have it all, but I can share strategies with you that work when you have to do it all from scratch or with what seems like nothing. If you find yourself nodding and saying *yes*, just know that you are not alone in this and, most importantly, you will overcome.

This book is for the military parent who must deploy, the parent who must stay behind and hold down the fort, teachers and childcare professionals who work with military children, civilians who support military families and readers who are curious about how to raise and nurture children who have military parents. The book is crafted to show raw experiences, share gems of wisdom, give guidance, offer strategies, and to cheer you—the parent, spouse, grandparent, family member, or caregiver raising a child with a military parent or some military background. The content of some chapters is also relevant for parents and families who are not affiliated with the military community.

INTRODUCTION

GROWING UP. DREAMING FAMILY DREAMS. I was born and raised in Ghana, a beautiful country in West Africa. I spent most of my childhood alone, starting from a very tender age. I lost my biological father when I was still very young. My mother, a widow who could neither read nor write, had to work many days and nights traveling across the country and crossing the borders of Ghana to other neighboring African countries as a tomato seller in order to put food on the table and a roof over our head. Prior to living alone, I lived with my maternal grandmother, my aunt, and my mother's friends. When I was about eleven years old, my mom could finally afford for me to come live with her at Alajo, a suburb in Accra, the capital city of Ghana.

Living with my mom for the first time really meant living alone in a large compound home environment where other parents helped raise the neighborhood children. We had our own room but shared basic amenities. On the compound, I saw different people. Old women and men. Young men and women. Teenagers. Children. Babies. Christians. Muslims. Non-believers. Men who went to work and women who stayed home and sold commodities. There were many family dynamics as well. There were families with both parents and children, families with parents, their children and other family members they had adopted as their own children, and there were single moms like my mom and our own family situation.

It was quite a busy compound house, with every family buried in their own chores and lives. I easily made friends with the other girls and I enjoyed playing *Ampe* with my new friends. Ampe is an exciting and easy Ghanaian game that requires two or more players, usually girls. You do not need any equipment for this game. When playing Ampe, the lead player and another player both jump in the air at the same time clapping two hands and thrusting one foot forward during the jump. If both the lead player and the other player shoot the same foot forward, the lead player wins a point. However, if the feet are different, the other player becomes *it* and gets to play against the remaining players. We were a group of girls who usually lined up during this game. We continued playing moving down the line until we were tired, or we heard our parents or guardians yell our names to come home and fetch water or eat dinner. Many homes did not have pipe-borne water in our deprived community. We would go to the houses of our neighbors who could afford to install water pipes to fetch water in buckets and carry it on our heads to our own homes for cooking, bathing, and washing clothes or dishes. We did this daily or every other day, depending on our family size.

On the compound, I also admired seeing the other girls with their parents or guardians. One day, another girl who was older than me named Gina invited me to church. Her parents did not go to church, but I would go with her on Sundays. This was where my Christian foundation was laid.

I must admit that as a young girl, it melted my heart to see other children live with their families in large compound homes that housed extended family members in the neighborhood. Life seemed not only normal but to be a haven for the children of those families. There were grandmas, grandpas, cousins, uncles, and aunties. Everybody that mattered in life. Seeing other children with their families at church, especially on Sundays, was a beautiful thing for me.

But I must also confess that at this stage of my life, I had lots of questions about my own background and family circumstances. These unanswered questions and harsh realities gave rise to me envisioning what kind of life I desired for myself when I grew up. So, I dreamed daringly and prayed fervently, not only with righteous rage weaved with unexplainable pain, but also with fat faith and huge hope. I would say that out of my many dreams, my most cherished desires were based on what I saw and admired, for what I thought *should* and *could* happen in my life. One of those revered dreams was having a place to call my own home and forming my bona fide *family* when I grew up.

Not only did I dream, I also prayed. I read. I spoke to mentors. I asked questions. I volunteered to look after children so I could just have a sense of how people raised their own children and to see the dynamics of modern-day families. I remember writing in my journal one day: *I did not choose my current family situation, but I have a choice and what it takes to create the family and home of my dreams.*

I smiled when I wrote those endearing words. I was hopeful. I was not sure how and when it would happen, but I wasn't worried, either. I was at peace with myself just dreaming, envisioning, and trusting that it would happen. Somehow. Someday.

Years later, when I said *I do* to my high school sweetheart who had just enlisted to serve in the United States Navy, I had no clue how that was going to significantly impact the kind of family I would be able to create. And what it would be like to grow and nurture a family *together* but also *alone,* for the most part. I know single parents are amazing, just like my own mother did in her own way and style. But when you have not chosen or embraced being a single parent, you look at it with a different lens.

CHAPTER ONE: CREATING YOUR HOME

Home is where your story begins.
—Annie Danielson

ABROAD. NEW APARTMENT. EMPTY SPACE. *No shipment of Household Goods.* Yes, my first real home as a wife was a beautiful and large two-bedroom apartment on a military base in Japan. It was an empty space with no household goods shipped or in sight.

When we got married, my husband still had to go through Accession training, known as *A school* in the Navy, where he would receive technical training in his field and finalize his orders at the end. After A school I could be included in his orders and travel and live with him at his new duty station. Up until that point, we were not sure how or when I would join him, due to many factors. First, I was still living in my home country, Ghana, with my family, but I was also eagerly planning and preparing to relocate to the US to be with my husband.

We met in high school in Ghana and were friends when we were still teenagers. A few years later, he relocated to join his family in the US. His family moved to the US when he was young and we have always joked that his parents left him behind with his grandmother when they were first migrating to the US so that we could meet. When he left, we continued our friendship, which later blossomed into a long-distance romantic relationship. Later on, when we decided to get married and settle down, we weren't sure how things would work out because of his Navy career and our respective locations. We sought counsel, prayed, and planned. We then mapped out a plan where he was able to travel back to Ghana after bootcamp for us to get married and filed paperwork for me to join him later after the marriage ceremony. Nothing was certain at this point, except for the fact that we wanted to spend the rest of our lives together and start our own family.

It took faith, praying for guidance, and trusting the process. When he finally phoned me one day to tell me that the orders had been modified from *unaccompanied* to *accompanied*, we were both excited. This was the greenlight that I would be able to join him in Japan for our overseas tour. However, his household goods had long been packed and stored at his parents' place in the US while he was in basic training.

My husband arrived in Japan a couple of days before I did. I was moving from Ghana and he was traveling from California. After checking into the squadron and going through the Area Orientation Brief (AOB) class, we made an appointment at the family housing office. We were given a two-bedroom apartment and were both thrilled. We quickly went to the hotel and packed our few personal belongings to move to the apartment. It was quite a walk. We did not have a car and hadn't met many people yet. Thankfully, we were two youngsters who were strong enough to carry our own luggage and our new comforter set.

When we arrived at the apartment, I stopped in my tracks and thought for a moment, *But what are we going to sit or sleep on?* I cast a worried look at my husband. Truth be told, we had not thought or talked about it. Clearly, there was a lot of new information to assimilate from our AOB class. Plus, we had many adjustments to make. We had been apart for six months and he had left barely two weeks after our church wedding. Prior to that we had been in a long-distance relationship for many years.

The transition was quite complicated, and relocating from Ghana, for me, was a whole process to go through and a bubble of emotions to deal with. I had been very anxious waiting for the spousal visa paperwork to be approved. I was not sure what I was doing and wondered if the same high school boy I knew before had changed or not, but I was happy and ready to take a leap of faith for the next chapter of my life. I will admit that leaving my family, my friends, and my collegemates behind was hard. Dropping the life I knew and taking on something I was not familiar with was a bitter pill to swallow. The future was so uncertain, but I was very hopeful. I remember closing my eyes tight in the airplane when I was traveling to Japan to be with my husband and telling myself that it was time to take the bull by its horns and take control of my life. I also strongly believed that God had good plans and thoughts for me, plans of good and not of evil, to give me a future and an expected end. I believed that in the end, everything would work out.

Since my husband did not ship any household goods from the States, we were not eligible for temporary household goods, either. More so, we were both very new to the dynamics of the military life and serving overseas. We did not really know who to ask or talk to at the time. And we were one broke couple at the time.

We finally located the Navy Exchange store on base and bought air mattress, bedding, pillows, a few cooking utensils, and some groceries at the commissary. I remember both of us just sitting down on the bare floor in the empty space and enjoying our meal on disposable plates and cups. The floor was cold, but our hearts were warm towards each other. We were happy to be together. *Finally!*

We were grateful for our apartment. I knew we would make it work, but I had no clue how or even where to start from in creating our first real home as a husband and wife, one that would welcome and house the children we planned to have.

The next couple of months I had two major goals: put our home together and look for work. I searched and read about budgeting, creating, designing, and keeping a home. I wanted to create a Godly home where we would both feel loved and wanted. A haven. A place to rejuvenate after a hard day's work. An environment where dreams could be made.

In my book hunt, the one that really stood out for me was titled *A Woman After God's Own Heart* by Elizabeth George. The book was eye-opening and educating as far as what Christian wives needed to take into consideration when making a home. She talked about how to create a nurturing home environment that is beautiful and honors God. I also brainstormed and journaled. I painted on paper the kind of home environment I wanted to create. I drew pictures of exactly how I wanted my home to look. I colored and played with moving around drawings of furniture and designs around on my paper.

The most important aspect of a home that I knew I wanted was for it to be a sanctuary for us to relax and rejuvenate. I also wanted a place where we would both feel loved, feel peaceful, and be nourished with fresh food and homecooked meals.

So, I went to the home store to look around and get some ideas, write down prices of furniture, and select certain colors and styles. I compared brown, black, and gray couches, for example. I also looked at leather versus cloth couch options. I sat on each of them to see how comfortable they were. My husband touched them to give his opinion. I was able to buy a fake plant, a wall clock, and a rug to begin with.

Before checking out, I dug through a pile of wooden plaques to hang in our home. One sign with the words *Home is Where Our Story*

Begins hit me hard on the head and sank deep in my heart and spirit. It resonated with what I have always believed. I have a strong opinion that we each have our own unique story, one that is first shaped by our home environment, then by our schools and community.

The other wall hangings with homey phrases I saw in the store were:

Home Sweet Home
This is My Happy Place
Happiness is Homemade
Charity Begins at Home
Home is Where the Heart Is
Home

As you can probably tell, I picked the sign that read *Home is Where Our Story Begins* because it echoes strongly with my personal beliefs about having children, nurturing children, and growing a family.

I believe that:

- Children first learn to receive and give love at home by bonding with family members
- Children learn to trust and to feel secure in a home environment
- Children learn healthy eating habits at home
- Children learn important values, such as trust, kindness, forgiveness, and responsibility at home
- Children learn to respect and be respected at home first
- Children will learn to love themselves, feel confident, dream, set goals, and believe in themselves as they see their parents pursue their goals.

In short, home is where all of our stories begin—good or bad.

So, I walked home with my sign and a big smile. That was a decade ago, but it was the starting point of creating my own real home and family.

The very beginning.

The debut.

It was exciting, intimidating, and just maybe I was overthinking it. We all do sometimes, don't we?

CREATING A HOME ENVIRONMENT WHERE EVERYONE THRIVES

A home should be an environment where everyone thrives. A happy place for everyone. A place where everyone feels a sense of true belonging. A place where each member of the family is loved, cherished, respected, and given a chance to nurture their own ideas, dream new dreams, and pursue their goals in life. A home is not necessarily perfect. It is not super-duper clean. A home is not rigid, with thousands of rules to follow. A home is a just place where you can be yourself, create yourself, and grow yourself. A home is a place that flows with authentic love, allows mistakes so you learn and grow, and embraces you as you are. Let me add that it is the people in the home that make it a home and contribute to how it is supposed to be for everyone.

With my personal family situation, my vision is creating a home where we all can flourish and thrive.

Myself. My husband. Our children.

I also want anyone who enters our home to feel the love of Christ and smell the sweet aroma of love, joy, kindness, hope, and peace. To help me execute this, I recorded this in my journal:

I want to create a home environment where each of my family members—myself, my husband, and our children—will grow, thrive, and be nurtured. A home where they will feel loved, cherished, appreciated, joyful, and peaceful.

A home where dreams come true.

A home where you can be who you really want to be.
A home where you can feel safe.
A home where you can be emotionally naked and be confident.

DESIGNING YOUR HOME ENVIRONMENT

Designing a home environment where each person thrives, including you, starts with the art of design. Your home should look appealing and have a personal touch and a unique taste. I use different strategies to create the home environment that I dream of.

For example, I select colors based on how they make me feel. I choose dark brown leather couches instead of black. The color brown is mild, close to nature, and tones down brighter colors in the home environment. I actually find the color brown calming as well. I pick gray colors for rugs. Gray is another calming color. I use woven baskets in the living room as storage bins. I keep blankets, stuffed animals, and soft pillows in the baskets. This works for my family, especially when we are doing a movie night or story time in the living room. We each treat ourselves to our favorite blankets. The girls add or switch out their favorite stuffed animals from time to time.

I buy wall hangings and I have photos of each family member and place them in the different areas of the house. I like to display photos of all of us together as a family at different times in our lives and from various special occasions. I make sure to display photos that include other family members, like our own parents. I have wall décor, like mirrors and abstract wall paintings. In our living room, I add a natural plant to one corner, a play area for the children, small fish tank, and a boat shaped bookshelf that houses our favorite books so it is easier for us to grab a good book and start reading. In addition, I have my favorite signs like *May This House Have Joy in the Morning and Sweet Dreams at Night* staring right at you when you turn from the sofa and when you get down the stairs from the bedroom.

My kitchen area is a little different. On my dining table I have a wooden bowl of fresh fruits like oranges, apples, and bananas, and I switch them around every week. The apples and bananas are colorful to brighten our moments and also a great motivation to snack on fresh fruits. I have seen my children snack on them rather than ask me for juice boxes and crackers all the time. Some weeks I just have a fresh pineapple sitting on the dining table on its own and I use it to remind my family members to stand as tall as a pineapple. I tell them to be sweet on the inside and always wear their crown.

I like to switch out different colored throw pillows on the couch, and adjust the signs for the different months or seasons. For example, I have signs that simply read:

Eat.
Bistro.
Meals and Memories are Made Here.
This is My Happy Place.
Happy Wife, Happy Home.

Across from our dining table is a sign that details our family rules: *Pray. Love. Be Kind. Forgive. Be Real. Say Sorry. It Is Okay To Make Mistakes.*

On the refrigerator we usually have artwork by the children from school and family photos of grandparents and other extended family members that we do not see often. We also place our memory Bible verse of the week there so we can remember and memorize it.

My bathroom is slightly different. I have just one sign that says, *Be Still* and a basket that contains a Bible, devotional guide, travel magazines, military spouse magazines, and a coloring book. You never know when those will come in handy. On the days I find myself breaking down in the bathroom, there is a survival kit right there to help me breathe, reassure myself, and compose myself so I can carry on. Yes, I have my breakdown moments at different times and days. The stress and struggles of the military lifestyle is real. Some days I feel overwhelmed with my husband being gone for a long time. Other days I am really exhausted getting my children to and from school, supporting my children's soccer and ballet practices plus helping them with their homework and the million other things I'm trying to juggle alone. Living abroad and on an overseas tour, many days I miss my family. It also tears my heart to see my new friends move to a different place. I am just a normal human being who has to wipe down tears of children who miss their Dad and must give them hugs and reassure them that Daddy will be home soon, all while trying to hold in my own sadness and frustration.

In addition, I sometimes have breakdowns during PCS moves, which are stressful times in the best of circumstances but are especially hard when I have to do everything on my own because he is out on deployment. So yes, having a survival kit of items that calm me works for me and I choose to keep it in our bathroom. And, perhaps most importantly, I have discovered that it does help us not to be on our phones or tablets when we're in the bathroom but rather read something Godly.

The next places in our home that I put together with care are the children's rooms. I have three children, one boy and two girls. My son is eight and my daughters are six and four years old. Decorating each of my children's room plays a major part in nurturing them, helping them to learn certain key values, building their confidence, and significantly supporting them to flourish and thrive. It is for this reason that I have a sign that hangs on the wall of my son's room that reads *Every Good and Perfect Gift Comes From Above*—James 1:17. Below this sign are different photos of him at different periods and events in his life: soccer practice, basketball tournaments, and Taekwondo testing times. There is another photo of him on top of Mount Trashmore in Virginia Beach having fun at the park with his Dad. I want to remind my son that he is a good child, even though he drives us his parents crazy sometimes. I want him to understand that he is a perfect gift from God. As a gift, we must love him, take care of him, and teach him the way he should go in life because some day we will stand before the great judgment seat of God to give an account of the things done while in body to include how we treated our son, nurtured him, and released him to the world.

Posted on the wall near his bed is also his vision board and projects he proudly completed in school. As he sees his work, it boosts his confidence, and as he sees his vision board it sends a reminder to his brain to work on those skills he wants to learn or master. My children loved the idea of vision boards and have fun putting together their own vision boards at the beginning of each year. A vision board is simply a collage of images, drawings, words, or anything that serves as a reminder of the dreams you want to achieve. Introducing vision boards to children is a great way of helping them talk about what they want to do, skills they want to develop and why, and most importantly, helping children learn the habit of setting goals and taking small steps to achieve them even at an early stage in life.

Putting together a room for a teenager or older boy could be slightly different. Notable key points to consider would be your budget, space, the personality of your child, and your expectations of how the space must be used. Most importantly, involving your child in the whole process of designing his room is key. Bear in mind that confidence and privacy is a big deal for teenagers.

Since teenage or older boys need space for learning and completing homework, creating an inspirational study corner, to include a desk and sizeable bookshelf, cannot be ignored. Add a touch up to the room with wall photos of his favorite athletes, cool collections or hobbies. Tennis rackets if they like tennis, guitars if they like music, or balls if they like soccer, baseball, or basketball are great ideas for inexpensive but fun decorations. Whatever their interest, you can use it to help decorate. In addition to all of these design ideas, knowing your child's favorite colors and adding a piece of furniture with that specific color can do magic in keeping him comfortable and feeling at home. Using neutral colors is better for older children or teenagers, as they do not want to feel like little children when you only use very bright primary colors.

However, in the case of young girls for example, making them feel comfortable by designing a visually appealing room with the space you have is very important. In my own situation, since both my girls are under ten years old, we decided to keep them in one room for now so they can bond more and enjoy playing together even though they are at each other's throats sometimes. Each child still has her own space in the one room. For instance, they each have their own bed and photos of them on their side of the room. In the closet, the space is divided for each of them to keep their clothes. Honestly, their current closet is tight, but we make it work by frequently cleaning out clothes they have outgrown earlier, rather than keeping them for years when we do not need them.

The girls chose shades of the colors pink and purple for most of the things in their room. They do have a dark pink curtain and a gray, fluffy Japanese rug. On their wall is a wall painting of flower petals. They also have artwork completed from school and daycare that they are proud of and taped to the wall. They have their vision boards on the wall and I hang photos of them hugging each other and playing together, and photos with their brother and us. There is one particular artwork from school for my older daughter that talks about who she is and what makes her unique that she really likes to talk about that we decided to keep as part of her collection in their room. Toward the corner of their room is a basket full of their favorite bedtime story books and stuffed animals.

My friend has a sixteen-year-old daughter named Rachel. Her room décor looks very different from that of my little girls' room the last time I visited them. When I asked Rachel what she liked most about her room and why she likes to spend time there, she shared that having a large bed with her favorite comforter set makes her feel happy and comfortable. She showed me her little space in the corner of her room where she likes to lay or sit and listen to her favorite music, color, or read to relax and calm down if she is having a low day. Rachel does not have many wall hangings, but she does have a study desk, a piano, a stylish table lamp, a fluffy rug, a walk-in closet, and a space for her cat. At the end of the day, it is whatever makes your child feel comfortable and makes them love hanging out in their room that matters.

Every family is unique. Choosing to design your home environment will reflect what your style is as a person. For instance, a family that has furry family members will design their environment slightly different than families that do not. Families with older children or other older family members will have a different kind of home setting. What is paramount is touching the lives of the people in your home environment with what speaks to their hearts and the things that spark joy, spur love, and ignite creativity.

END OF CHAPTER REFLECTIVE QUESTIONS

What is your ideal home environment? Do specific colors or articles appeal to you? Why?

_____

_____

_____

In what ways do you think your own home environment can support your efforts in nurturing your military child and in helping your family flourish and thrive?

_____

_____

_____

Look around your current home environment, what would you do differently? Would you add, eliminate, or substitute anything?

_____

_____

_____

CHAPTER TWO: BECOMING A PARENT

Children are not a distraction from more important work.
They are the most important work.
—C.S. Lewis

EACH AND EVERY ONE of my fellow military spouses I have met have their unique stories of becoming a parent. In the military world, pregnancy and childbirth is usually a calculated move. At one of our duty stations, my friend and next-door neighbor told me how she had to calculate when the ship would be pulling out and work around getting pregnant so that her husband would most likely be home close to the time the baby would be born. My colleague at work also shared with me how during her entire pregnancy she had to juggle work and other responsibilities, including caring for her two other children. Her husband arrived a day after the baby was born. When we were stationed in Japan at Atsugi, my close friend Michelle drove herself to the hospital on another base when she went into labor, which was about forty-five minutes away from her home and our base. This is familiar story for many military families stationed overseas. Michelle's mom flew from the US to help but could not drive. Her mom and little girl were at the back seat while she drove to the hospital when she felt it was time. Her husband had worked things out with the command and they had agreed to fly him back in time to witness their first child together. As the clock ticked, baby Isabella was impatiently swimming her way down. Michelle's mom was more nervous than Michelle herself. When I later asked my friend why she did not knock on my door so I could drive her to the hospital she reminded me, "You were also heavily pregnant at the time and alone as well!" We both laughed as we recounted our experiences. Both of our husbands were on the same ship and were deployed at the time. Michelle's husband arrived a few minutes before the baby's head was seen.

My own story in becoming a parent is no different. In my case, I remember peeing on the pregnancy test stick in the bathroom one day with my eyes tightly closed as I prayed. I felt anxious. Would it be a plus sign or a minus sign? Would it matter or not when I was not even sure how I was going to survive living overseas all by myself and trying to have a baby alone while my husband would be deployed for most of our overseas tour?

My husband and I decided to wait to have children when we first got married so we waited for two years before trying. We needed to adjust and learn the dynamics of living together as a husband and wife first. I also needed to settle down and find work. As I sat there, a tsunami of questions rushed through my mind as I continued to pray.

When I finally opened my eyes, I stared at the stick. It was the plus sign. It meant I was pregnant! I was happy and he was too. With a husband who deploys a lot, you only have a window to try and get pregnant before he leaves.

So, for the most part of 2012 he was out there defending and protecting us and our country, and I was baking a baby. Before I knew it, my belly was growing fuller. My body grew larger. My face swelled. My neck darkened more than ever. I had morning sickness every hour of the day for five months. I thought about moving to my neighbor's apartment. *What if something happened to me while he is gone?* I squirmed at the thought. I finally decided to stay in our apartment. I was working full time with school-age children at the youth center as a programs assistant. I loved my job but walking became very difficult for me at the later part of the pregnancy. I remember waddling like a penguin when we picked up the children from school and had to walk them back to the center for after-school care. Luckily, I had great support from my colleagues and my supervisor at the time was very understanding.

Deciding to have children is a big decision, depending on your unique situation or marriage relationship. It affects your body, your budget, and your home as a whole. It can be very exciting, but also confusing and very demanding. Planning and having a strong support system, especially if you're stationed overseas or have just moved to a new duty station is very key. The support system can be reaching out to your ombudsman to see what groups and help can be available to you.

Informing your supervisor, especially if you have complications or if your job demands heavy lifting, can help protect you and the baby. Some organizations are able to respect some accommodations if you work with your supervisor or talk with your human resource representative. To help the deployed parent connect more with the baby in your womb, you can take photos of your growing belly and photos of the baby during ultrasounds and share it with them. This is a personal choice, as some cultures are very sensitive to sharing such images. You can also write letters or send emails talking about how you are feeling and coping with the pregnancy. Keeping a journal helps you track important progress and details that you might want to send to your partner or spouse. In addition, you can involve the deployed parent in your plans when the baby arrives even when they are not there by sharing with them your ideas and design for your nursery, things you are buying, and ideas for baby names. Giving the deployed parent an idea of events happening in their absence, like baby showers and gender reveal parties, (if you choose to engage in any) are other examples of great things to share with the deployed parent. Your goal is to make them feel part of the process as much as possible and feel connected to the unborn child to the best of your ability.

FOR THE NEW MOM

Becoming a parent changes everything! Let me just say it: becoming a parent changes a lot of things . . . I mean *everything*, to be honest.

As the mother who will carry the babies in your womb, your body, shape, form, and state of mind will change in *a lot* of ways.

I remember standing in front of the mirror a few weeks after I had my first child and looking at my body with a shocking gaze. My physique wasn't the same anymore, no matter how many times my mother had tied my belly, bathed me with hot water and towels, rubbed shea butter all over my body, and prepared certain foods for me to eat in order to regain my energy and retain my body. The tying of my belly was a tradition for new moms back home in Ghana that my mom urged me to take advantage of. Basically, she used an old cloth and wrapped it around my belly and back area and then tied it into a knot. The idea was to help me lose my belly pouch quicker and to heal faster. My mother believed that there were still remains of childbirth fluids and blood in my womb and that the more she tied my belly, the more those fluids were flushed out of my body during those first few days after childbirth. Some days she tied my belly all by herself. Other days she convinced my husband to use his male muscles, so it was quite tight. Honestly, it was something I endured from two people who are endeared to my heart. I do think it actually helped some, but losing my belly pouch took time and effort. I had to eat healthy, exercise regularly, rest more, and give myself time.

I also remember that even though my husband had bought the treadmill as a gift for me and I had used it a few times, I still found myself staring hard at my new physique and fighting uncontrollable tears running down my chubby cheeks. I felt so out of shape and I broke down a lot.

My friend Karen told me how she could not take it when her husband looked at her and even came close to her few weeks after giving birth, as well. She hid her body. She noted that it took her time to take it in that it was okay for her body to change. That she was still beautiful. You are still loved and your new body, the scars from C-sections, and the stretch marks are all beautiful reminders of the little miracles you brought into this world. In my own experience, it took me time and grace to embrace my new body with love and gratitude.

If you are the attention-seeking type of person or the one who thrives on compliments, just like most of us, you are going to have to adjust your crown. When the baby arrives, the attention will now go to the child and *many, many, many* times people will stop and admire the baby and not pay much attention to you. Really. People are typically drawn to the smiles and beauty of a fresh baby. They will ask how the baby is doing or growing and show how much they love them. Fewer people—and sometimes no one—will ask how you are doing for a long time. You may even feel you are no longer loved, but that is not true. The world is amazed and stops to admire a miracle you birthed. Embrace the honor.

Time is damned precious. You will have less time to do all the important things you need to do, including using the bathroom. You may be rushing out to take care of the baby halfway through pooping, especially when you hear him or her cry. Most first-time moms fear something might happen to their children and that they have to be there at all times. Caring for a newborn takes all your time. You are on a twenty-four-hour clock with feeding, changing dirty diapers, rocking them to sleep, and repeating the same process again and again for a good number of weeks and months. Some babies eat and sleep well. Other babies are colicky and cry a lot. Some moms will heed to the advice of experienced moms and try to enjoy the process and sleep when the baby sleeps so they can retain their energy and be in a better position to continue standing the baby watch. Other moms, especially if you are a first-time mother, will go by the book and want everything perfect, including a super clean home. Believe me, that was me when I had my first child, but I had to learn quickly to drop all those expectations so I could thrive.

Life is busy in the military home, especially when those babies start entering your abode —with or without permission (birth control doesn't always work). You will feel overwhelmed. You may question what you are doing and may even doubt the fact that you are taking good care of your child, even when you are doing your optimum best.

As a new mom, you will not have enough sleep any more for a *long, long* time. My friend, Natalie, tells me how she still wakes up in the middle of the night to make sure that her children are in bed. Her children are thirteen and ten. I never really thought about worrying over older children until I heard about teenagers leaving their homes in the middle of the night with their friends partying.

You will forget a lot of things. I mean *a lot!*

You may go through post-partum depression multiple times if you have multiple children. People may not know what that is, understand you, or will tell you that the depression is in your head. You can get a lot of help from your team of medical professionals, but you may not get any support at all if you do not recognize it or talk to your doctor about how you feel.

You will be out of gas a lot of times mentally, physically, and emotionally. This is when you will need to make the time to sleep, shower, exercise, and eat, even if you have just a little time to do it. You will have to improvise and engage in some exercise (after your doctor gives you the okay) for short periods of times at home for the first few months. Discuss with your doctor which simple exercises you can engage in.

As a new mom, you may feel cheated, as everyone in your home sleeps and snores at night and you are the one up nursing a baby. But that is totally okay. That is the sacrifice all mothers make. Talking to your spouse for help, especially if you decide to bottle feed, is a great start, but sometimes duty will call him to stand watch, or go on the ship, or deploy to Afghanistan. Really, he or she can deploy anywhere at any time, and it may just be you and your child or children.

Trust me, it is not all gloomy, dark, and hard work. It can be filled with pure joy as well. You will fall deeply in love with the new life that you just released. I remember waking up in the middle of the night and admiring my children when they were so tiny and sleeping soundly. Peacefully. They looked beautiful. Those were miracle moments for me. Tears of joy rolled down my face. I would actually remind myself how wonderful I was, allowing myself to be used as a vessel to bring life into the world. I would feel so proud holding them. When I had our third baby and one day the other two joined me and the baby on the bed, I remember asking myself if these three little human beings really came out from my body. You may find yourself in wonder as well. If you wake up in the middle of the night or at dawn remind yourself that you are the one who carried your baby in your womb, pushed them out, and is now nurturing them. It is a wonderful achievement and a blessing, so praise God for it.

FOR THE NEW DAD

Becoming a dad while serving in the military is not for the faint hearted. I watched my own husband grow from a teenager to a young man, then to become my husband and the father of our children. I also watched him fill with excitement at first about becoming a father, and saw jitters painted all over his face as a new dad, and finally witnessed the pride and joy that lit up his face when he saw and held each of our children in his hands.

I call my delivery day the *big show* day. I am grateful my husband was right there holding me as they stuck the giant needle into my spine for the epidural. I thought I could not take it. I remember him prompting me with the guidance from the nurse when it was time to push. He translated everything into Twi, our local language from Ghana. Trust me, when I was in labor, I could not understand anything in English or tolerate any talking from anyone. I wanted to be spoken to in French or Twi. Luckily, he was there to speak to me in Twi. I also remember seeing him cut the umbilical cord of all three of children with vim and later he told me how the nurses let him bathe his babies in the nursery at the hospital.

Being a dad is a huge responsibility that comes with pride and maturity. There will be days when you think you've got this and other days when you think you don't know what you are doing, especially if it is your first child. Trust the process, be patient, and be gracious with yourself, as well as your spouse, as you both journey on the path of parenting together.

Some cities and hospitals provide informational parenting classes for new dads that are very helpful. There are a good number of books written by dads for dads that could arm you with critical information and knowledge that can give you the right perspective on parenting.

My husband preferred to go the traditional, old-school way. That involved figuring it out on his own, reading a few blogs or articles online, and consulting his parents when he needed help. Stories and experiences shared by a few friends and colleagues gave him some helpful tips as well.

As a dad, it is very important to know that during the first days and weeks of the baby, the mother of your children is going to need all the love, help, and support that you can give her. You will need to be more sensitive and caring, reassuring her that she is still beautiful, as she is likely to go through tons of emotions. The bottom line is, she will be aching in body, mind and spirit due to fatigue and sleep deprivation.

I am grateful that my husband took up some baby duty at night when our children arrived. He was able to get a few days off, and also sometimes his work shift changed and that helped a lot.

My mother was there to help us, but as the father of the baby, those bonding moments were critical. He typically offered to watch the baby so I could sleep about three to four hours straight at night and not worry about wet diapers. When we decided to introduce the bottle, he would be the one to feed, change wet diapers, and take care of the baby so I could get up to six straight hours of sleep. My mother and I would then take over during the day with everything else. I felt much better, stronger, and in a better mood to care for our newborn. He, on the other hand, felt more connected to his children. With my mother being present, my husband and I were able to go on walks some days. During these times, we talked, we laughed, and we quarreled, but we bonded, as well. Most days we were overwhelmed as new parents and we did not feel like talking, so we just held hands or argued and came back home, but we were grateful we could get out of the house and breathe.

When I gave birth to my second child, my mom came to visit and help but had to leave three weeks after her birth to attend to personal matters. Our friends on our base, whom we call family, supported us in many ways. My friend, Brenda, and her husband kept our baby so we could go on a date night. Some of our friends also cooked for us. Others offered to do a grocery run, and my friend, Elisa, offered to braid my hair for me so I could look human again. The support was enormous.

Preparing for deployment as new parents is essential. There will be many unanswered questions and a bubble of emotions. In our case, I sensed the resentment of my husband as he prepared for deployment while the babies were still very young. My husband was resentful about the fact that he would be gone many days and months and would be the one missing out seeing how our children would grow. When I was pregnant with our first child, he was also worried that I was by myself and away from family and support while he was in the middle of the sea for several months. Making the time to talk about how we each felt, what we could do to keep him in the loop and reminding each other that deployments eventually end helped us. When he deployed, I emailed him photos of the children every day, shared the things we did every day at home, and told him about any changes I saw in the children as they grew. I also mailed any artwork to him that the children did while he was gone, and we talked about the new children that moved to our block. My husband shared how he was on the moon when I shared that our daughter said *Dada* while pointing to his photo.

SURROGATE DADS & ADOPTIVE PARENTS

If you are a surrogate dad or adoptive parent, people may wonder how to approach you or ask about your family dynamics. Being gracious and helping people who might be working with your child or taking care of your child understand what kind of parent you are can be helpful. Some people will have their own opinions and others will be more curious about your unique family story and life.

When I first met three-year-old Brianna, for example, her beauty and smartness struck me. I could not guess that she was birthed out of surrogacy. I remember seeing her very attached to her dad. I was one of her teachers. A few days later, I met her other dad and I was a little confused, but then it finally made sense: Brianna was being raised by two males. One of them deployed a lot in the year. It took time for me to learn the dynamics of Brianna's family. Her dad was graceful enough to tell me more about his experience with surrogacy. The term was quite new to me, so I quickly searched for its meaning and learned quite a few things.

Surrogacy is a legal arrangement where a woman agrees to bear a child for another person or persons who will become the child's parents after birth. In Brianna's case, her surrogate mother was from India and her dad was from the US. Brianna's dad, Mathew, narrated with excitement and pride the process and his experience. As direct-care teachers working in a childcare center at the time, some of the information shared helped us understand more and helped Brianna to settle in. We also observed and planned classroom activities to meet her unique needs and feel more accepted in our classroom learning environment and program as a whole.

My other experience with adoption was meeting four Black children with White parents on a military base overseas. I remember the bright smile of the parents and the manners of the children. Honestly at first, I thought they were their babysitters, but then for a long time I saw both parents together and it clicked one day. The parents were quite older. I learned later that the couple's biological children were grown and they decided to adopt their new set of children. Their story and kindness melted my heart.

As a parent raising a surrogate or adopted child, your child is going to find themselves in an environment with other children who may have similar or totally different family situations. The key is to help your child understand who they are and fall in love with themselves. Your children are going to need you to assist them in gaining some self-confidence, as well. Being open and giving them a chance to play and learn with other children is going to help them thrive. Other children may look at them differently, ask them questions, and have their own opinion. Teachers in schools and daycare centers are usually trained to practice an all-inclusive program and classroom, but, speaking from experience, there is always that one child that may pick on your child. Practicing open communication and helping your children stand up for themselves through a positive approach is a great way to arm your child for the unknown.

END OF CHAPTER REFLECTIVE QUESTIONS

What factors are most important to you when you consider (or considered) having or adopting children?

_____

_____

_____

What is your own experience of childbirth? Did you get any help or support? How did you manage the changes to your body?

_____

_____

_____

As a new parent, what would you say are some of your unique challenges? What advice do you have for other new parents?

_____

_____

_____

CHAPTER THREE: ROOTS AND WINGS

There are only two lasting bequests we can hope to give our children.
One of these is roots, the other, wings.
—Johann Wolfgang Von Goethe

I GREW UP KNOWING OTHER people better than I knew my own parents. For the most part of my life, I lived with my grandparents, my aunt, my mother's friends, alone, or with my sisters from the other womb.

My widowed mom traveled most of the time to find work so she could provide for me and my brother. As a result, she was gone frequently and for long periods of time. I remember feeling resentful sometimes when I did not see her and then even feeling resentful for the few times she was present. I also remember getting used to it at some point and eventually not caring about it at all. It was not until I became a mother myself that I fully understood why she had to be gone a lot. It made sense to me that as a mom, your greatest pride is to see your children well fed, housed, educated, and happy. My mom paid more so I could get a better education from elementary to college level. Back home in Ghana, elementary education is not free at the time of writing this book. In addition, my mother sent me to private schools for a large part of my elementary schooling. It was when I became an adult that it began to make sense to me why she worked a lot and was gone that much. I was finally able to let go of the bitterness of living in different homes and not seeing my mother as much as I longed for her, something I had been praying for a very long time.

Living in different homes has gracefully shaped who I am in many positive ways, and I am grateful for that. I learned how to serve others, cook, organize, clean, and maintain a neat home environment. These are important skills and values that I personally believe one should have as a person and even more so as a woman, mother, and wife. Most importantly, living in different homes led me to envision and pray for the ideal home for my own children where there is pure love, lots of laughter, and plenty of room to be nurtured, to make mistakes, and to dance like no one is looking.

In my own situation, I am happy that I learned to develop some roots through the unconventional way that I was raised. Some of these roots were seeds that were planted by people God placed at every stage of my life. They include my Sunday school teachers, my godfather, my Scripture Union camp officers, my classroom teachers and lecturers, the parents of my friends, my stepsisters, and my brother when I met them later on in life, and also my bosses, supervisors, colleagues, and other people I came into contact with as I volunteered and worked. Reading also exposed me to the key strategies of developing strong roots. Since I had to figure out a lot on my own at a tender age, I had to dig for the information on how to make life work through Christian literature and many other self-help books on personal development, professional development, marriage, caring for children, success, and careers. I can testify how these roots have helped shape my life as a young lady and as an adult today.

Children need deep roots and wide wings for life. In effect, giving your children deep roots and wide wings no matter what your family situation looks like is one thing you cannot ignore when raising your children. There are three key things to take into consideration to help arm your children with the right information, forge the right identity about themselves, feel grounded in love, and feel confident enough to take on the world.

THREE KEY STRATEGIES TO DEEPEN ROOTS AND GIVE WINGS

Having a vision for your family, sowing seeds of faith, and modeling values that are important to you are the three key strategies that can help your children develop deep roots and give them wide wings for the world out there.

For example, as Christian parents, our goal is to pass down our Christian faith to our children and to model Godly values in our family and home. In addition to that, we expect our children to flourish and to thrive in every aspect of their lives, to include being responsible and ethical citizens. It is for these reasons that in my own parenting journey, I use different techniques to help us deepen our roots and grow wings as a family. My children are still quite young but when my spouse shines at work or I get a good report of how my children are doing when we go outside, I can tell they are developing roots and growing wings that I am proud of. In addition to that, when my children stand up for themselves or protect someone else, when they apologize for being in the wrong, and when they show a good attitude and resilience in a negative situation, I see that they are exhibiting what we model as parents at home. I am confident that they will shine and become who they want to be. I am also hopeful that when they fail, they will choose to rise stronger. And that when they make mistakes, they will learn and be victors, not victims, of any situation life throws at them.

In our family, our root-deepening and wing-growing techniques vary. The popular ones we are currently using include vison boards, memory verse jars, gratitude jars, and confidence boosting containers.

HAVING A VISION FOR YOUR FAMILY AND SETTING GOALS TOGETHER

Growing your family requires you to first have a vision and a goal for yourself and for your family. Your vision is a mental picture of who you want to be and what you want to achieve as an individual and as a family. For example, do you foresee in your mind's eye a home environment where children will thrive and a place where dreams will come true? I have found that creating vision boards for myself and as a family help us identify specific goals, boost our confidence, give us something to work on and look forward to, and help us grow stronger together as a family. This year I was able to involve the children in the process for the first time. Each child identified what they thought was important and what skills they each wanted to master so that as a family we can be the best, reach our goals, and celebrate each other's success.

To start, my husband initiated a conversation one day as we drove from basketball practice about how Max, our son, had performed. My son has been learning to play basketball since he was three years old and we could see that he was improving on his skills each time. We commended him. Our daughters laughed, clapped, and cheered him in the car as we drove. We then asked him if he wanted to continue playing and what skills he thought he needed to learn to do better. If he wanted to stop playing too, it was okay with us. He named learning to dribble and practicing shooting higher with a tone of excitement. My husband let him know that he would be watching a basketball game that evening and that LeBron James (top American basketball player) was playing, so they could watch it together to see how the professional basketball players play, if Max was interested. He also mentioned that they could go to the basketball court near our house later and they could practice, if he was up for it. "Yes!" my son exclaimed, mostly because of the TV part, I think (we do not typically let them watch a lot of TV at this age). Before the conversation ended, my second daughter chimed in, "But Daddy, I want to learn some cool ballet moves, too," and my third daughter added, "And I want to swim in the water!" I sat there with all these thoughts and a zillion questions on how in the world I was going to support these goals, knowing that in exactly three weeks my husband was going on several short detachments for the next couple of months, which would be crowned by a very long deployment soon after. Though my heart smiled at the conversations happening, in my head I said to myself, *Girl get it together! How are you going to make all these happen in addition to everything else you do, including working full time and writing?* However, I managed to add to the conversation, "Sometimes, when you have something that represents what you really want to learn or improve, having your own vision board can help. So how about you create your own vision board sometime this week?' They concurred. They had seen one before but we had not fully talked about it yet, so I saw that this would be a great opportunity to introduce it to our children.

That week, we re-read some of our children's books that talked about confidence, dreams, and goals. Our favorite picks were the books titled *The Little Engine That Could* by Watty Piper, *Dancing in The Wings* by Debbie Allen, and *Dreams Come True, They Just Need You!* by Mike Dooley.

That same week, we made a trip to our favorite dollar store in Japan. We bought everything we needed for our vision board projects, to include poster boards, markers, glue, stickers, and scissors. The children enjoyed picking their own supplies and choosing the colors of their own markers.

Throughout the week, we talked about our goals as a family as we ate dinner or drove to and from school as part of our usual conversations so we could finalize our boards.

TIPS FOR CREATING VISION BOARDS WITH CHILDREN

Involving the children in creating a vision board can be exciting and challenging at the same time, but it is worth the effort. Giving your children a head start in life with the idea of setting goals prepares them better for the future, makes them more responsible, and boosts their confidence. There are different ways to do that.

1. Start by talking to your children about what they like to do and why, and what areas of their lives they would like to improve, if they are old enough to comprehend. It is okay if they do not know what they want to do yet. With time

and practice something can drop in their heads or hearts someday. Put down any ideas that come up as you engage in this activity at every stage.

2. Share your own goals and vision board if you have one already. You can use the internet to show them some other examples. If you do not have a vision board, this could be a great opportunity to make one.

3. Read children's books about goals, self-identity, self-confidence, and skills improvement to introduce them to the concept. It will also get them excited. Our favorite books around this topic include *Stand Tall, Molly Lou Melon* by Patty Lovell, *She Persisted* by Chelsea Clinton, and *Jojo's Flying Side Kick* by Brian Pinkney. Picking the right kind of books will depend on the age and interest of your child or children. Researching on Amazon and Google and reaching out to other parents can give you ideas of what great books you can use, as well.

4. Shop for items for creating their vision board together. If your children are old enough and can get to the store and buy the supplies themselves, encourage them.

5. Pick a great time that works for you and your family to work on the vision board project. For us, it was a Saturday morning after our favorite pancake breakfast.

6. Sit and create together. Help your children cut if they are young and need help. In the case of older children, it is a great idea to create your own at the same time, as this can be a great bonding time as well. If your child is a teenager and would prefer to create alone and show it to you later, do not stop them.

7. Talk about how and when you are going to reward yourselves or celebrate when you attain any of the goals listed, drawn, or demonstrated on your vision board. In our own case, we decided we will do a quarterly check-in to see how we are each

doing and as a family. We love a sushi-go-round restaurant in Iwakuni, Japan called Hamazushi, so it is a royal treat when we nail a goal. If we all do very well, we will give ourselves a small family weekend trip to Beppu, our favorite steamy island in Japan, while we are still here.

8. Use the time creating the vision board to talk about what success means to each person and what to do when goals are not met.

9. Assure children that it is okay if they do not reach a milestone or hit a goal or even when they fail. It is important for children to learn that failure is part of life and that life is not always pretty or glamorous, or always about winning. Sometimes we must fail in order to learn and develop success muscles.

10. Hang their vision board where they can see. It can inspire them. In our home, we hang it in their rooms. Our family vision board is in our kitchen. I also have one that is digital this year and I explained to the children that it is easier for me to look at it, especially when I am not home and I need to work on some of my goals.

For a start, we plan to keep our annual vision boards throughout the years to come so we can see how we have grown and how much we have worked to improve certain life skills, attain certain goals or review the goals we never reached. Each year, we will be able to look back at the old ones and see if we need to adjust our goals or delete or add more, based on the old ones.

SOWING SEEDS OF FAITH: MEMORY VERSE JARS

As a Christian family, the second most important strategy for deepening our roots is sowing seeds of faith in the minds and hearts of the people in our home including myself.

I became a Christian at a Scripture Union camp when I was still in high school. Prior to that I went to church and was very much involved in church activities. I was also a natural leader among my peers at school and church. I was a Sunday school secretary. I also acted and taught my peers memory verses and new songs in the absence of our Sunday school teacher.

As a child who started living by myself at about age eleven, I can testify that my faith in Christ and God's grace took care of the little details of figuring out life by myself in a harsh community and environment.

As an adult, I am still figuring it out and I know it is only my faith that enables me to keep it together when life turns upside down and does not make sense. And perhaps most importantly, I want to make it to Heaven and the only way is when you believe in Jesus Christ. It is for all of these reasons that sowing seeds of faith in myself continually and in the lives of my children is of utmost importance to me. Creating memory verse jars where we learn at least one verse a month and then tuck them into a jar is helpful and keeps us going.

One common goal this year was that we wanted to grow our faith by memorizing twelve Biblical verses by the end of the year. We figured using memory verse jars is a tool that can help us reach that goal.

To create a memory verse jar, I use colorful paper and cut it out to the size that I want. Sticky notes do the trick as well. I pick the verse I think we need for that particular month. Sometimes, when we are doing a specific study at church, I pick a verse that goes with it. Other times, the children's Sunday school teacher may want them to memorize a specific verse and we just run with that. In certain cases, when we are going through something as a family—good or bad—we pick a verse that speaks to us and the situation.

I have also found that talking to my children about the importance of memorizing Biblical verses and getting them excited by giving them the opportunity to pick their own jars from the store or creating one themselves work very well when you are first introducing this strategy to your children. Some days, the children will be enthusiastic and certain days they will not. We have a reward system where we typically give certain treats, including dining at our favorite restaurant or going on a field trip to our favorite playground, when we meet memorizing our verses per month or quarter.

Apart from using the memory verse jar, we use other methods to sow seeds of faith in the hearts of our children. We have weekly family devotions, for example. We also encourage the children to read their Bibles. Right now, only my son can read, so he has a children's devotion that he usually reads in the morning in the car as we drive to school, or first thing when he wakes up if it is the weekend. I have a couple of the children's Bibles in my car and a couple of books. The days we miss family devotions, my son reads a children's Bible story as we drive. In addition to these, being part of our local church connects us with other Christian families with whom we share faith, friendship, and food every week.

In my own experience, volunteering at church and with other Christian groups, like Scripture Union-Ghana strengthened my faith when I was growing up. Taking up leadership positions in school, participating in extracurricular activities, and advocating for children's rights as a member of the Curious Minds (a media child rights advocacy group in Ghana) boosted my confidence, deepened my knowledge, sharpened my media skills, and connected me with various opportunities to be a problem solver and a younger leader who represented my home country in international fora during my youthful age.

As a parent with this background, I strive to expose my children to the realities of the world by reading different geographical and historical books with them so they can learn and understand the bigger picture of our present world. I also urge my children to support local charities and we volunteer when we get the opportunity to support our community.

MODELING IMPORTANT VALUES: GRATITUDE AND CONFIDENCE BOOSTING CONTAINERS

The third key thing to help with growing your family using the sowing seeds and deepening strong roots idea is modelling those values that mean everything to you as a person. Values are what you think is right or wrong as an individual. They are what you believe in and what defines how you live your life. Values could be passed down or developed by life experiences. They can also be taught intentionally. Some of my personal values include faith, prayer, gratitude, self-love, love for others, kindness, forgiveness, loyalty, courage, responsibility, respect, honesty, goals, dreams, determination, perseverance, empathy, positivity, open-mindedness, care, compassion, peace, and wisdom.

If you know me, you will identify at least one of these values in my personal and professional life. In raising my children, my chief goal is to help them develop some core values for their own lives and for who they will become in our family, community, country, continent, and their generation. As a mom, I strive to model these values at different times. For example, I apologize to my children when I find myself yelling because I am tired, grumpy, stressed, or I need their attention. My husband will apologize too when the children let him know or when any of us see that he is yelling.

My husband and I first started the gratitude jar long before introducing it to our children. As a couple, it is part of our New Year's Eve tradition to name our blessings one by one for the passing year and give thanks to God as we prayerfully crossover into the new year. To begin the night, I pull out the paper strips that I have kept throughout the year or sticky notes one by one and read aloud. They often read like this:

> *Grateful for another successful deployment.*
> *Grateful we are still alive and together, healthy and have our faith.*
> *Grateful there is a roof over our head.*
> *Grateful for our family and our home wherever we are.*

This is just to mention a few. My husband will nod to show that he agrees. It is mostly my handwriting on those sticky notes, as he prefers to keep his in his mind or write them down at the very moment we are talking. One night we talked for a very long time as our paper strips led to stories of how we grew up, the struggles we went through as children growing up, the hustle as young adults, the grind as a new couple, and the struggles as new parents. We talked about how God has brought us to now and about the growth, the maturity, and the blessings of family. We decided to try this exercise in gratitude with the children during Thanksgiving, at first. We know our children would listen when they saw the big golden-fried turkey on the Thanksgiving table. It worked. Truth be told, I like keeping this tradition regularly, especially when he is deployed. Sometimes I mail some gratitude sticky notes to him alongside the children's artwork that tell him how much we admire him and that he is our best hero out there. In my low moments, I remember to dig into the gratitude jar.

Confidence-boosting jars are similar to gratitude jars. They both work great in our home for the children and, honestly, for myself as well. I decided to introduce the concept when I figured my son had some low-confidence issues. It was a complimentary activity I did together with using the *Big Life Journal,* a growth mindset book, journal, and printouts that help children think positively, persevere, and believe in themselves. In the children's confidence-boosting jars, you will find simple notes like:

You are my best Meghan.
You are just great.
Give it your all today.
The sun is smiling down on you because you deserve it.
Be You. We just like how you dance.
You are my hero and our hero.
Boss lady is killing it.

Confidence boosting jars can be opened at any time—for a reminder, a discussion, or a quick pick-me-up. In our home, we open them when we are on weekend getaways or throughout the day, especially on the weekends or no school days. I personally like to open the jars as part of my *me time* routine alone with no children or husband. I pull some out while a candle burns away and there is a soft music playing in the background. The children are able to keep some in their rooms as well. My son likes to keep his under his pillow and my daughters like to post them on their door or the wall in their rooms.

END OF CHAPTER REFLECTIVE QUESTIONS

What does the word *values* mean to you and what are some values that are important to you that you would like to pass on to your own children?

_____

_____

_____

Do you have a family vision board? Why or why not?

_____

_____

_____

What are some family traditions that you would like your children to embrace and pass on to their children as well?

_____

_____

_____

CHAPTER FOUR: PLANNING AND PRIORITIZING

A child can teach an adult three things: to be happy for no reason, to always be busy with something, and to know how to demand with all his might that which he desires.
—Paulo Coelho

GROWING YOUR FAMILY BY HELPING them flourish and thrive is no small task, but it is an honor and a sacred duty. In effect, it is a process which essentially requires using different strategies to raise children to be the best they can be and nurture them to be good citizens and members of society. I call it *bringing up men of valor and strong women of faith who will be salt and light in our world by praying fervently on the journey of parenting.* Ultimately, it is a work of heart that takes dedication, commitment, hard work, and faith. Therefore, this calls for careful planning and high prioritizing. It takes careful planning for most people to welcome little ones into their lives, space, and home, and then to take care of a child's basic needs. For some mothers, it takes their health, memory, and even their lives.

STRATEGIES TO PLAN AND PRIORITIZE AS A BUSY PARENT

Children will keep you on your toes and caring for them can be stressful. As a mom and a military spouse, I find myself juggling many different things at the same time. I have felt overwhelmed caring for my own children and found myself drowned in dishes and diapers with no plan of escape. I have been exhausted and drained and felt sick in the process at the same time. And oh yes, I have had a series of meltdowns as I tried to raise my children, keep my home, pursue my career, and be an attractive wife at the same time. Many times, I felt alone. Lost. Unnoticed. If anything at all, I have learned to cheer myself up, keep cool, calm, and collected, and get moving. Trust me, oftentimes no one will care or see or understand your struggles, sweat, and sacrifices. No one will clap for you when you think you deserve a standing ovation and a deep bow. This is when you need to look yourself in the eye and remind yourself that *you've got this!* With prayer, you gain the grace, strength, and wisdom for the journey. Other times too, help will come in different ways and from different directions and you will have that one person who will care and tap you on the shoulder to affirm you.

Learning to do certain things in specific ways is what will get you through as a busy and sometimes messy military spouse and parent juggling everything and anything from PCS moves or closing and selling a home, to giving birth in a foreign country with little to no family support.

Let's discuss just three approaches to planning and prioritizing. *Identify what is most important to you.* The first step is to identify what is important to you as a parent and as a family. This should include growing your faith as a family, self-care, dining at home on fresh, homecooked meals, making sure your children are doing well in school, having your children participate in sports or extracurricular activities, creating memories together, engaging in stress-relieving activities, cultivating values, developing skills, and learning to be self-disciplined. The process of doing this include brainstorming, reflecting, praying, talking as a family, envisioning, trying, failing, and getting your feet wet in the process so you can learn what truly is important to you as a unique family. The practice can take time, so allow yourself space and time to figure this part out. Writing out my ideas, talking, and journaling has helped me identify those things that are important to me as a person, as a mom, and as the homemaker and the heart of our family. My husband remains the chief and head of our family. Since he deploys a lot, I make it a point to bring certain important things to him for discussion, confirmation, and concurrence, if need be.

Schedule your time to support what matters to you. The next most important step is to take stock of everything you do every day and how much time you spend on each activity. As a parent you will be responsible for feeding, cleaning, planning playdates and breaks, and making sure that your child gets what he or she needs to live and succeed in life. All the tasks you will be doing will consume your time. You will also need to carve out time for yourself, your spouse, other family members, your friends, work, school, and church in one way or another.

Taking stock of how much time you spend on each of these will help you identify what eats up your time the most. This will further help you determine if you need to give up on those things that consume your time but may not necessarily be in line with your family goals. And for the things that align with your goals, you must schedule them practically so you can execute them.

Personally, when I am trying to squeeze in time to take my children to practice or spend time with them, I put them down on my schedule. I make an appointment with myself in my planner or calendar. For example, as a military spouse and mom who works outside the home some days my schedule looks like this:

8:00 a.m.-9:30 a.m. — Meeting/Training
10:00 a.m. — Coaching session
11:00 a.m. — Lunch with Junior
12:00 p.m. — Gym
1:00 p.m. — Complete report
2:00 p.m. — Inspections

On a different day, my 3 p.m. to 5:00 p.m. afternoon appointment is ballet rehearsal for my daughter or basketball practice for my son.

In the same way, your own schedule will look different based on the kind of work you do or if you are a stay-at-home parent. What is most important is scheduling specific and important things, to include spending time with your child.

Clean and organize your home environment. Organizing is my go-to for help when I find myself running in circles in the morning and wanting to pull my hair out trying to look for underwear or a sock for my children. And it typically happens on days when you wake up tired, sick, or running late for school and work. To help minimize this, we organize and prepare on the weekends for the school and week ahead in our home.

Saturdays are usually the days I do most of our laundry, cleaning, and cooking. It is a major day and I get the children to help me clean and organize the house. They get reward points for their help and sometimes they earn a few dollars, too. Each child has a basket where they keep their underwear, socks, gloves, and hats depending on the weather or season. Each child also has a place I keep their clothes folded or hung and the children and I typically select clothes to be worn for the five days for the following week. I do the same for myself and my husband, as well (when he is home). I also do all the necessary ironing. When my husband is not standing watch, he helps with this part. My son is growing older and we have started showing him how to prepare for the following week by himself, so it is not super crazy in the mornings on in-person school days when they have a bus to catch or I have to drop them at a specific time before heading to work.

In addition, the children help clean the shoe closet and tidy their rooms as well. When I was a new mom, I decided on specific areas I needed to clean and organize so I could easily find a baby bottle, a pacifier, or diaper. As my children grew older, I got some help from them as I patiently taught and guided them on cleaning and organizing to make life easier for us. I found out that this makes them feel responsible, learn basic skills, value their personal belongings, and most importantly, they are able to get ready in the morning with few reminders and little support. This is because they typically know which clothes they can wear to school and where to find them. It is less stressful and frustrating when we keep this routine. I find myself not yelling or losing it in those rush-hour mornings.

Similarly, in the kitchen, we know where to find a cup or plate, spoons, what foods in the fridge are healthy breakfast, and what we need to keep for snacks. We are all on the same page for the most part on what to do when we finish eating. This includes basic cleaning up after yourself, scrapping your plate, and leaving your dirty dishes in the sink. With practice and consistency, this makes life easier for everyone in the kitchen.

It looks like lots of work at first, but it is worth putting in the effort. When laundry is folded and organized it helps children find their clothes easier. When the house and toys are organized it brings sanity to you. It also limits visual stressors.

I had to specifically explain to my husband at some point that walking into a clean home environment after a hard day at work and a busy afternoon with the children is very calming and comforting. This meant I needed my living room to remain as clean as I left it as much as possible, my sink relatively tidy, adult dirty socks and underwear in the laundry or a laundry basket, and my bed made on those days that he is home. With prayer, patience, and graceful reminders, I started getting help in that area, for the most part.

Every home is different, so I would say implement what works best for you. For example, my friend Laura is a single mother who lives with her fifteen-year-old daughter and she tells me that it is her daughter who does the ironing of her clothes and cleans the dishes. In likewise manner, if you are a stay-at-home-parent, you may not necessarily feel the need to pick clothes for the week or prepare meals ahead of time.

Create routines that work for you. I find routines to be helpful as I attempt to manage my time wisely, plan, and prioritize so I can grow and nurture my family. A routine is how you manage the sequence of the events of your day. It is basically what you typically do every day to keep your life and goals and those of your family's on track. For instance, you could have a routine of waking up at a certain time, brushing your teeth, taking a shower, eating breakfast, leaving home for school or work, completing homework, and preparing for bedtime. When I was younger and single, my routine was much simpler than when I settled down, got married, and started my family.

Let me add that when deployment duty calls for my husband to leave, our routine is different. In the same way, when he comes back that routine changes if there is any routine to keep at all. Honestly, there is really not much of a routine when he comes back from deployments, as it is a real struggle. Most military spouses can attest to that. You are not alone.

In our family, I can say that daily our routine begins with me. I usually wake up around the same time every day. On a good day, I am able to do my devotion, push in a fifteen-minute, quick exercise in my living room and prepare breakfast before I wake the children up. Some days it goes smoothly. Some days it is a different story. Some days there is a slight change as well, depending on what project I am working on like, for example, writing this book. Since I am a morning person, my morning routine will include an hour of writing before I start my day. At night, I need a routine that helps me get my hungry and tired children fed and bathed, their homework checked, and getting them prepared for bedtime. You set yourself and your family up for failure or success if you do not check your routine, adjust and readjust it to see what makes it better for you and everyone. Keep trying and working at it. The trick is to be flexible.

As an adult, my nighttime routine includes a time to wind down and some quiet time for me to reflect on the day. I typically drink tea while the lights are dimmed, the candles lit, and soft music plays in the background. Sometimes I pray. Sometimes I find myself crying because I am tired, feeling overwhelmed, missing my deployed husband, or something did not go right at work. I have learned to appreciate that this is perfectly alright as long as I am getting those emotions out in a positive way.

Our evening routines as a family involves calming activities before bedtime. Television, tablets, Nintendo Switches, cellphones, or any form of technology does not calm children before bedtime. As a matter of fact, research shows that electronics before bedtime stresses children and makes them take longer to fall asleep.

When I realized our children woke up in the morning sluggish, cranky, and seemed like they could not remember how to put on their own clothes, I had to look deep into what they were eating right before bedtime, which day of the week they typically experienced that, and also what activities we engaged in right before bedtime. I then readjusted our nighttime routines, and we had a conversation with our children about the changes, which included no electronics an hour before bedtime on school days, since sometimes the children have homework to be completed on the computer. If you work from home or your children are in virtual school, your routine will look different and that is okay.

I find certain calming activities before bedtime for children usually do the trick in preparing for a smooth transition to rest and relaxation for our family. Examples of calming activities that I have used in our home that worked really well with children of all age groups are:

- Reading bedtime stories
- Looking through family photo albums
- Drawing or coloring
- Playing family board games
- Journaling
- Working on puzzles together
- Creating origami or other crafts

We pick different stories from the library or the store, and sometimes we borrow from friends. About thirty minutes before bedtime, we gather and read. Some days, we read three books because each of my three children want their books read—even my son, who can read by himself. Sometimes, we have my son read the books, sometimes my husband reads to the children, but most times I read to them. Somedays, we talk about the characters of the book and other days we are too tired and just want to drift off, so we do little talking and more yawning when the reading is done.

Viewing our family photos is another calming activity before bedtime that works well for us. We like to travel down memory lane and remember all the things that have taken place in our lives, the places we have visited, and events that have been captured on camera. We just pick the family photo album and flip through the album and smile, laugh, and remember wonderful things that have happened to us before we go to sleep.

On a very busy day for me as a mom, especially when my husband is deployed, drawing and coloring is my go-to activity. The children have blank page books and coloring books. They can just retire to their bedrooms and color and draw whatever they want before they sleep. This gives me time to tidy up the kitchen or house before I go give them a goodnight hug and kiss before they fall asleep.

We love family board games. Our favorite ones are Chutes and Ladders, Candy Land, Pete the Cat board game, Monopoly and *Oware*. Oware is a Ghanaian board game that requires an Oware board and about forty-eight seeds or pebbles. The game requires two players who must sit at the opposite end of each other. The Oware board has two rows of six pits that have houses. Each player is the owner of these houses and controls the houses on their side of the game and can score on the houses at their end. You win when you are able to capture more seeds than the opponent. Players typically sow and capture seeds to win.

Involving your children in choosing the kind of bedtime activity is helpful in getting them to participate. They will also enjoy it more.

Be flexible and learn from what works and what does not. Just as it is important to learn and execute the strategies shared, it is also very important to be flexible. You need to learn to adjust to what works and what does not fit in your own unique lifestyle and family dynamic. I would also suggest that you give it time when you try any of these strategies. When you introduce new routines to your family or children, it usually may not work at all or works well for the first time and then does not work the next and then it does work for a long time. Assess your own family situation. Being mindful of the fact that family members have their own strengths and weaknesses will help you in being flexible with your style and strategies. Taking notes of the strides you make is what does the trick.

Ask for the help you need. Need someone to take care of the children for a couple of hours so you can breathe, especially when your spouse is deployed? Ask your friend or neighbor, or hire a sitter. If you have just moved to a new duty station, speak with your ombudsman to see what kind of help or support is available for you. I am very guilty of asking for this kind of help, but I am grateful I have friends who give it to me before I even ask. If you have family members around, ask them to give you a hand. Forget about what they will think of you because a lot of times they actually want to help you out. Our culture makes it look like you are a weakling when you admit you need help. Do not fall for that. Our grandparents had five, six, and even ten children in their time because they got all the help from their sisters, aunties, and every other person who lived near them, like the compound where I grew up. They understood that it takes a village to raise a child.

END OF CHAPTER REFLECTIVE QUESTIONS

What does your family routine look like? Share which routines work best for you and your family.

_____

_____

_____

What strategies do you use to plan and prioritize what matters to you and your family?

_____

_____

_____

List any games and activities that you have used before bedtime that your family has benefitted from the most.

_____

_____

_____

CHAPTER FIVE: PRAYING FOR AND WITH YOUR FAMILY

Rule for happiness: something to do, someone to love, and something to hope for.
—Immanuel Kant.

I LEARNED TO PRAY FOR everything when I was growing up. I prayed for potable water, electricity, and food while living in our compound house back in Alajo. I also remember praying for my mom to return home safely every day when I was child. She told me stories of car accidents each time she came home, and I saw her cry a lot when she lost some of her friends during those car crashes. Most importantly, I prayed passionately for her to be converted for several years before she became a Christian. As a wife and a mother today, I strongly believe in the power of praying fervently for yourself and over your family.

Every morning, my children and I hug each other tight and pray together before we open the door and hit the road to begin our day. Sometimes we just hold hands as we stand close to the door and pray. Our prayers are usually short, like: *Dear Lord, thank you for this wonderful day. Thank you for waking us up. Be with us as we start our day. Be with Daddy wherever he is.*

If any of the children have a school project, we pray and ask God for help and guidance. If anyone of us is sick, we pray and ask God to heal us. Daddy is often gone, either for trainings, short detachments, or long deployments, and a lot of times we truly do not know where he is. I do, however, know that he is in the middle of the ocean, but I try not to emphasize that around the children, as they might get scared or have weird dreams about the sea.

When I first started introducing praying with the children, we would typically pray in the car on our way to school. Each child took a turn and prayed. I would be the last to pray sometimes, or the first. I remember the children arguing over who prayed first the last time and whose turn it was. Our children fight and argue all the time about stuff like this, so honestly, I would rather they argue about praying. I would step in and remind everyone how we need to be kind and gracious even when we are upset about who always prayed first, last, or not at all. I would also use these teachable moments to discuss the importance of forgiveness, tolerance, and giving everyone a chance.

During this time, I saw the growth and maturity in our children. I remember my middle daughter always mentioning everyone's name and asking God for specific things for them. For example, she would pray and ask God to help her brother learn how to pay attention in class and to listen more. She would also pray that God would help Grandma to understand their English and for them to understand Grandma's language. This was when my mom was living with us and helped take care of them. My mother spoke Buli and Twi (Ghanaian local languages) with them all the time. My daughter would also pray for her Daddy, for me, and for her little sister.

My favorite part was when my youngest daughter prayed. She

was learning how to talk then so she could not find the words or say long prayers. She would basically say: "Dear God, Daddy, Daddy, Daddy. Amen."

That was her sweet and short prayer. This was especially when Daddy had been gone for a very long time. Other days, she would say prayers like, "Dear God . . ." then would mumble, saying words we did not think existed or we didn't understand at all. In those prayers we would hear each of our names. Mind you, she would go on and on and on until I said, "Amen," especially when we had arrived at school.

At the time of writing this book, I am doing things a little a bit differently with our praying style during weekdays when we have little time and also the drive to school is much shorter than where we used to live. We would actually say short prayers out loud at the door and then we would do our Bible study in the car. My oldest is the one who can read, so everyone takes out their Bibles and chooses one story. My son then reads them aloud. Since I am the one driving, I mostly listen and ask questions that prompt discussions. Sometimes we are able to tie in how that affects our relationships with our friends, our day, projects, and what we are expecting God to do in and with our family.

To be honest with you, when I wanted to start praying with my family, I did not really know where to begin and how things would go, especially with the children. My husband and I took baby steps and were just natural with the process and sincere about our feelings. We started with short Bible studies and prayers when we woke up on Saturday or Sunday mornings before our special pancake breakfast treat. These were the times when he was not deployed. We also always prayed and thanked God before we ate. And when I was struggling to squeeze time for my personal quiet time with the children all by myself, I would just sit in the couch with my blanket, Bible, and journal. I would read in the middle of the chaos. I would kneel in front of the couch and pray, and I would read my Bible as they played. With time, I saw that my children were picking up certain Biblical ideas and it made it easier when I had to explain why and how to spend time with God praying for yourself and the people in our lives. When I introduced the memory verse jars to the children, we could link it to praying and studying God's word.

In sum, the Devil is on a mission to attack families, to tear down the very thing that holds society together. It is for this reason that I spend time on my knees every day lifting up my family in prayer. It is also for this reason that I teach my children to pray alone and together as a family, and why we pray for the people we live and work or go to school with. As a military spouse and mother of three myself, I understand how each family dynamic is different. Carving out your own time and trying different techniques on different days and times is what I have found helpful. Whatever your style or family dynamic is, make it your attitude to stay prayed up always because life will most likely always give you more than you can handle, and you will need to learn to kneel alone and also with your family.

END OF CHAPTER REFLECTIVE QUESTIONS

What is your personal experience in teaching your children to learn how to pray?

_____

_____

_____

What strategies have worked best in helping your family stayed prayed up?

_____

_____

_____

Which area of your life do you think you need to focus on praying for?

_____

_____

_____

CHAPTER SIX: INTRODUCING A NEWBORN TO OLDER SIBLINGS

I love these little people; and it is not a slight thing when they, who are so fresh from God, love us.
—Charles Dickens.

WE HAVE THREE WONDERFUL CHILDREN and each of them entered the world at their own times and style. The first two were fashionably late and the third one arrived bright and early. And the best part was that all three of them were welcomed cheerfully into our home in a different manner and fashion. My son was the one who arrived a day later than my due date. I remember being so huge and could barely walk. Luckily, my mom was here to support us. I am grateful that at that time I did not have to worry so much about cleaning the house, maintaining the nursery, and eating homecooked meals.

I was in labor for about eighteen hours. The Chinese movie titled *The Raid: Redemption* was what finally did the trick. I remember watching the movie on the couch with my husband and my mother. It was a wild movie in my opinion, with a lot of suspense loaded with an ocean of thrills. I was forty weeks plus, but since my contractions were not short intervals I chose to stay home and enjoy a movie with my family. Shortly after the movie, I went to bed. I made my normal trip to the bathroom at dawn. I wiped after peeing and lo and behold there was blood. That was the sign I had been waiting for.

I had read so much that I was not even sure if I was contracting the way I was supposed to in order to start my journey to the hospital. But the blood was my cue. I quickly woke my husband up and we sneaked to the hospital, which was about forty-five minutes away. Upon arrival, I was examined and told to eat breakfast, take a walk around the base, and then come in for another examination, but I found I could not eat. I walked around the base hand in hand with my husband. We talked, we laughed, we argued, and we hugged. We also squeezed each other's hands. We were ready to welcome our first baby into our world and our home. My husband was super excited that it was a boy because we were going to name him after my husband.

When we finally returned to the hospital, I was admitted. The epidural procedure was the scariest part for me. I also remember feeling like I would die from those painful contractions before the epidural. From my labor room I could see my mom sitting across a corner just outside the room I was in. I saw her lips open and shut as she looked up at the same time. She was praying quietly in the spot where she sat. Beside my bed was my husband, standing close and holding my hands and encouraging me, whispering, "Babe, you got this, you can do it."

I finally felt hungry, so I requested some food. The nurse brought me ice chips and I looked at her like she had lost her mind. During my birthing brief earlier, I thought ice chips meant frozen potato chips or something. I shook my head when I saw the ice. I felt like puking, so I requested a bowl. I threw up so fiercely before I finally pushed the baby out.

It was 4:48 p.m. when my son finally made his way out of me after forty-one weeks and eighteen hours of being in labor. I heard him cry, the first cry of my precious baby. The doctor threw him onto me. He looked like jelly, but he was big, fresh, and beautiful. I looked at him and then looked up at my husband and felt tears rolling down my tired cheeks. They were tears of joy, love, and pride. I couldn't believe I had produced a baby. Another human being just came out of me. I was not watching a movie and I was not watching some other person. It was yours truly and for me that was a freaking awesome miracle! Giving birth was a blessing from above that I am truly grateful for.

I stayed in the hospital for three days and I was discharged to go home. Since my son was our first child, we did not have to worry about meeting and competing with any other children. I spent most of the time preparing myself mentally, taking care of myself physically, and planning financially for him. The presence of my mother made a great difference.

Baby, do you want milo? Introducing my two younger daughters to my son took a lot of effort. First, we started encouraging my son to listen to and look out for the movement of his little sister in my belly. He was quite fascinated by it most of the time and sometimes tickled my belly.

Second, we involved my son in the process of preparing for the arrival of his little sisters. I went baby shopping on some days with him. He was still quite young but when I picked something for the girls, I would show it to him and tell him that it was for the baby in my belly, pointing to my stomach. He would smile or nod or just ignore me sometimes.

I must admit that shopping with my son was a challenge, so I only did a few trips to the store with him, especially if I could leave him at daycare or with my husband. One time, when I was heavily pregnant, he ran around in the store and hid behind clothes and I could not run after him or even find him. Another time, he threw a bad tantrum and ended up rolling around on the floor in the store. Not only did he create a scene for the shoppers, but it was hard for me to get down and pick him up because of the size of my belly. I could not fight back the tears in my eyes that day. You can call them pregnancy tears. My husband was deployed then so I did not have anyone to leave him with when I needed to go grocery or clothes shopping.

My husband did his part, too, in preparing my son for the arrival of another child in the home. My husband put together the baby cribs with my son, for example. I saw the pride and excitement in my son's eyes as he helped.

When we arrived from the hospital with my oldest daughter, we placed her in the living room and asked my son to come look at his baby sister. I remember seeing my son standing there staring in awe at his sister. The next few days he wanted to share everything with his sister. It was a battle to make him understand that the baby was too young to drink *milo*, for example. Milo is chocolate and malt powder produced by Nestlé food company. You can mix milo with hot water or milk to produce a beverage that both children and adults can enjoy anytime. In our home, we typically drank it for breakfast or before bedtime. I drank it a lot when I was pregnant with my children.

My son's favorite thing was asking, "Baby do you want milo?" He did it with all seriousness whiles pointing his sippy cup to her. I also remember that when we went for walks, he wanted to be the only one to push the baby stroller. He did not want me or my husband to touch the stroller at all. We would joke and laugh after the walk.

Introducing our youngest child to our older children was a little bit different. Basically, we just looked at the new babies and talked with them. We would say things like "Hi Maya, this is your big brother Max. He is excited you are here." We would smile as we talked and the baby either looked, smiled back, or did nothing at all, especially for those very first few days and weeks. As time went on, the youngest children would coo or smile big or raise their hands in the air when we talked about their older siblings to them.

Our friends and family also supported and helped in many ways to introduce our youngest children to the older children and to make the transition easier. When I gave birth to our youngest child, my friend and colleague Audra brought over baby gifts for my new daughter and small gifts for my older children, so they got some attention, too. My other friend, Ellen, took my older daughter on a special outing just for her and my husband took our oldest son to a dinosaur show so both older children still had some attention.

In conclusion, introducing a newborn to older siblings and vice versa is a series of exciting things that involves both parents and your community of supportive family and friends. It is a journey that starts when you get pregnant. It is also a process that, if done well, creates a unique and strong bond between siblings. And finally, it is quite fulfilling to go through it together as a family.

END OF CHAPTER REFLECTIVE QUESTIONS

What is your own experience in having more than one child?

_____

_____

_____

How did you introduce your children to each other? Did you do anything special?

_____

_____

_____

Do you know of any friends or family members whom you can support them as they strive to give attention to all children?

_____

_____

_____

CHAPTER SEVEN: GOING THROUGH DEPLOYMENTS WITH CHILDREN

How lucky I am to have something that makes saying goodbye so hard.
—A.A. Milne

IT WAS LATE SEPTEMBER 2012 in Atsugi, Japan. My son was only three weeks old when we both had to say a tearful goodbye to my husband as he returned to the ship, hoping he would make it back for our son's first Christmas. Honestly, it was a long summer with the pregnancy, so I was quite relieved when he was flown back to witness the birth of our son, our first child. It was a pretty difficult period in my life. I was loaded with emotions. First, I was excited about my new bundle of love, then I was also disappointed that I had to be the one to care for the baby alone. But I was not the only one going through a variety of emotions. My husband was frustrated that he could not see his baby grow during those early periods of his life.

Deployments are unavoidable stressful events for military families. Every spouse and parent have their own unique story about their experience. No matter how much you read or learn, you will still feel the heat of deployment.

Going through deployment without children was different from going through deployment with a child. Before I had children, I could hop into my car and just drive somewhere when I was losing it. I also could easily find the time and energy to engage in different things in the community, including volunteering, but I was also bored for a large part of the time. When I had to go through deployment with a child, it was a different tale. Not only was I consumed with caring for a newborn, but I found myself drowning in diapers and drained from washing dirty dishes. The lack of sleep and rest was also killing me, especially being overseas with family far away. I could not say I was bored this time. I was damned *busy!*

As a parent, it is critical to find ways to handle deployments so you can be in a better position to support your children. Taking time to learn about deployment duration and planning what you are going to do during that time is very important. It is also necessary to have your support system in place. Your support system can be your go-to friends and family when you start feeling the stress of deployments. These are folks you can talk to, people who can give you a break from your children, spend time with you, or just listen to you talk.

I have also personally found deployment periods as a good space to work on my personal and professional goals, such as losing weight, getting a new job, taking college classes, learning a new skill, writing, or traveling.

It is important to note that your children will feel stressed and show different behavior patterns during the different stages of the deployment. I have observed that usually two weeks before the deployments children exhibit anxiety, anger, frustration, and confusion. During this time, they tend to communicate to the adults in their lives, mostly parents, childcare providers, and teachers, by exhibiting challenging behaviors such as rebelling, throwing tantrums, hitting, biting, screaming, and crying a lot. Older children may have difficulty following directions or focusing on schoolwork, and their grades may slip.

Bear in mind that this is a normal part of the deployment phase and is sometimes an inevitable experience. Taking care of yourself, arming yourself with information and tools, having a strong support system, plus knowing how to respond and support your children during this difficult time is very important if you are the parent who is left behind.

STRATEGIES TO HELP THE DEPLOYED PARENT

Take memorable items with you to your ship or your new place of deployment. For example, take special artwork of your children, photos of times spent together on trips, at the park, cooking, or attending events together. You can also keep video records of silly times together. In our home, my husband sings and dances with our children when they are making their pancakes or baking. We both have the videos, and we play them over and over.

Make yourself notes of special days—birthdays, school events, and extracurricular activities your children participate in. Then purchase cards and small gifts that you can mail back to your child. Children love to see their deployed parents sending them something thoughtful in the mail like a card, a book, a small gift, or handwritten notes.

Make every effort to stay in touch with your little ones. Phone calls, video chats, emails, and handwritten cards and letters are some examples.

During tough times, remember that you are out there not just because of the love you have for your country, but you are really out there because of your child and your family.

STRATEGIES FOR THE PARENT WHO STAYS BEHIND

For a good amount of time, you will be confused as a parent. You will wonder if you are doing well and you will also doubt your parenting skills. Deployments will make it better or worse.

Just like the deployed parent, you are going to need lots of memories to keep you going. Collect specific photos, games played together at home with the deployed parent and make it a habit to play together with your children.

Stay in touch with the deployed parent as much as possible. I remember sending lots of emails, even when I had not heard from my husband. He told me how he appreciated me writing to him all the time even when I had not heard from him due to his operations schedule.

You are also going to need a support system. This should be a circle of true friends and family members who can help you or give you a break from the children. People who would just listen to you vent and people who can spend quality time with you when your spouse is gone.

I spoke with my friend, Bridgette, and she told me how she and her husband love to travel and read when they are together. They pick a few books together before the deployment and they aim to read the same book at the same time at their different locations during deployments. They have email conversations about what they are reading and that helps foster closeness for them.

As a couple who loves to travel, they also pick a country they would love to visit and task each other to research and read everything about the place, especially exciting things to do. They email each other about what they found and the first things they want to do or places they want to visit when they can finally make it there together.

My husband and I like to watch certain television shows and movies together. To confess, he has watched more TV shows and movies than I have. I would rather read a book or write one. I can also reveal to you that when I watch the shows, my perception and interpretation of the story line is very different. So, when he is deployed, I watch certain shows or movies and we have email conversations about them. He amazes me about remembering and even explaining more about the plots each time.

I can tell you that deployment is no joke at all, and no one gets used to it, depending on how you see it. You may get used to certain routines when your spouse is deployed but not necessarily everything that comes with it. Be patient and know that just like anything else, deployments have an end, and you will have your loved one back home.

STRATEGIES TO HELP CHILDREN COPE WITH DEPLOYMENT

Your resilience and how you handle the stress of deployment will affect the children in so many ways. Children will have meltdowns, will rebel, and you might see low grades in school. You are going to need to use different strategies to help your children go through this phase.

First, make time to talk to the children about deployment as a family before, during, and after deployment.

Assure children that the deployed parent still loves them. Remind them of memorable times like family vacations, board games time, mealtimes, and family movie times, for example. Even if they are young, talk to them, show them pictures, and be there to comfort them.

The deployment we went through in 2020 was the most challenging one for us as a family because of COVID-19. My husband did not get the break that they typically get during the deployment. The children and I engaged in different projects to keep us going and also to share with my husband. First, we started and maintained a garden for the first time. We simply went to the store and bought planters and seeds. Each child picked whatever they wanted to grow. We mowed the grass in the back yard ourselves versus getting someone to do it for us. We picked a spot for the garden, placed our planters, distributed the dirt, sowed the seeds, and watered them regularly. We also took pictures, and my son kept a journal of how the seeds grew. I remember sharing with my husband proudly via email that the children and I really did not know what we were doing but our seeds were sprouting, and the garden was blossoming. Some of the plants also died, but in all it was one specific project that the children wanted to show their dad when he returned from deployment.

Have children make cards and write letters and help them send care packages to the deployed parent. My son started keeping a journal titled *Dear Daddy,* where every week during deployment he would write and describe how he was feeling, what he did, and what he plans to do when his dad returned from deployment.

Make it a point to connect your child with other friends whose parents are deployed as well, so they can talk and share. This will help children feel and understand that they are not alone in this.

My children and I have found it very beneficial reading different story books that speak to us a military family. Our favorite books are:

Dear Baby, I'm Watching Over You by Carol Casey
Daddy's Boots by Sandra Miller Linhart
My Mom's Boots by Elizabeth Gordon
I Love You Near and Far by Marjorie Blain Parker
Sometimes We are Brave by Pat Brisson

I Love You Just the Same by Erica Wolf

While You Are Away by Eileen Spinelli

Pilot Mom by Kathleen Benner Double

I Love My Daddy by Sebastien Braun

Don't Forget, God Bless Our Troops by Jill Biden

Brave Like Me by Barbara Kerley

A Paper Hug by Stephanie Skolmoski

The Wishing Tree by Mary Redman

A Year Without Dad by Jodi Brunson

My Daddy is a Hero by Hanna Tolson

END OF CHAPTER REFLECTIVE QUESTIONS

How do you talk to your children about deployment in your own home?

_____

_____

_____

What strategies have worked for you in learning to cope with deployments alone or with your children?

_____

_____

_____

What projects could you do during deployment with or without your children the next time your spouse deploys?

_____

_____

_____

CHAPTER EIGHT: HELPING YOUR CHILDREN TRANSITION TO NEW DUTY STATIONS

Sometimes you will never know the value of a moment
until it becomes a memory.
—Dr. Seuss

I AM WRITING THIS CHAPTER from Iwakuni in Japan. Specifically, in our newly constructed three-bedroom duplex in the Atago Hills Housing Community. Atago Hills is off-base military housing that is about fifteen minutes to the main base. Iwakuni has been our home for the past two years and my family absolutely loves the place, the people, and the fresh produce.

This tour meant we were attached to Marine Corps Air Station (MCAS) Iwakuni even though we are a Navy family. This particular base has also served as the home for other Navy families who were transported from Naval Air Station Atsugi in the Kanagawa prefecture in 2017. The base also accommodates civilians and local contract workers, plus some Japanese military personnel.

In my experience, this base is a unique community in its own way for various reasons and has a special place in my heart. First, Iwakuni remains an isolated base in a remote area, sitting in a farming a community. We see farms on our way to the base. The lotus farm during the summer was a beautiful sight and we often liked to stop there and catch our breath.

Second, it remains for us our third duty station together as a family. Even though this is our second tour in Japan, our experience here is completely different from what we have previously known.

As a family, the first time we had to move with the children to a new duty station they were very young. My son was two years old and my daughter was just five months old. We were moving from overseas back to the USA. The children did not really know what was going on then. My son understood that we were going to a different place and asked a few questions. The main issues to deal with were the long flights, sickness, and how we as the parents were managing the stress of moving so we could better take care of them.

The second time we moved was much more difficult, especially for my children. My son was now six years old, my oldest daughter was four, and my youngest daughter was one and was traveling for the first time. My son was also already in elementary school and my oldest daughter was in preschool. We were moving from the States back to Japan. I was moving and traveling alone with our three children. My husband had taken the lead and had already checked in a few months before into our squadron and was at sea on deployment when we arrived on the installation.

Even though my children were young, they remembered their friends in school and in the neighborhood and asked if we would ever see them again. They also cried leaving behind my mom and their Grandma, who was staying with us, and talked about some of the places we loved to visit in Virginia Beach and in Florida.

For most military families, a Permanent Change of Station (PCS) move usually happens every two to three years, and in some cases within a year depending on the situation. Some spouses choose to remain in one location whiles the Active Duty service member moves around the different duty stations. Some families prefer to move together. From experience, handling the move together as a family whether one parent is moving or the whole family is moving is very important.

Let's delve into some ideas on how to help your child transition smoothly to a new duty station.

Talk to your children about the transition. A great way to start is by discussing your upcoming move with your family, especially if your children are old enough to understand. Name the place and give the children an idea when the move is likely to happen. Initially, children may be excited or show signs of anxiety. Your goal is to identify those fears or anxieties early enough so you can work through them together as a family. Help children understand that you know and care about how they might be feeling. Assure them that you are going through the transition together and that you are there to help them through it.

Look for ways to learn about the area- landmarks, culture, food, and places of interest. Your next most important thing is to find different ways to learn about the new place. Read about it. YouTube videos may help and Google may give you tons of photos of the place. When we were going back to Japan, we started reading more books about Japan with our children. We also talked about the Japanese famous children's *Anpanman* character. Anpanman is a Japanese cartoon for children. The character is a round-headed superhero who must protect his friends from germs. And finally, we made it a point to visit sushi restaurants in Virginia and Florida before we left for Iwakuni. It was a great way of giving our children a foretaste of the new country we were heading to. Our children asked questions and we answered as much as we could and this helped with the transition.

Connect your children with other children or families and teachers in your new location. With social media, it has become easier and faster to connect with other spouses and families on other bases. Almost all bases have Facebook groups, and you can connect with other parents before you even get to the new duty station. You can find out about childcare options, sports, and other activities in advance and set up video calls with children the same age as your children, so there will already be a connection forming. This is especially beneficial for older children. Sometimes just knowing one person can take a lot of pressure off.

In my own experience, joining the Iwakuni Spouses Facebook page before we moved to Iwakuni in 2018 was extremely beneficial. I was able to get information on housing options, how the children's room might look and the general layout of the base houses. Other military spouses reached out to me privately to give me more information, answered questions to the best of their ability, and provided further resources like phone numbers and names of people to talk to about certain specifics. As a spouse and a mom who was moving by myself with three young children, it was extremely helpful to have those connections, information, and support.

Youth sponsorship is also available on some military installations for older children moving to Navy bases. The main objective of the

Youth Sponsorship Program is to coordinate a smooth transition for children. This sponsorship program helps children meet new friends with their peers who understand the military lifestyle. The youth sponsors support the transitioning process by answering any questions they might have and helps them settle in the schools and communities.

Explore the new area together. New areas are always exciting to explore. Look for local newspapers or magazines that may have places of interests listed and involve your children in the planning and explore these places together. My children and I like to take selfies and then make scrapbooks afterwards. We keep a family photo of the places we explore in our living room and sometimes we just look back at the photos and cherish those moments. This is a great way to fall in love with the place.

Go through emotions together. In your new place, sometimes you will miss your former home and the friends you left behind, and you will wonder if you will ever love this new place or find good friends. Children go through it and so do adults and parents. Acknowledge that these feelings are real but also understand that it takes patience, effort, and time to fall in love with your new home, create memories, and make new friends.

END OF CHAPTER REFLECTIVE QUESTIONS

Share your own experience with frequent PCS moves, alone or together as a family.

_____

_____

_____

What strategies have you used to support yourself and/or your children as you moved to different locations?

_____

_____

_____

What other ideas can you explore to make the transition a little bit smoother as you move?

_____

_____

_____

CHAPTER NINE: TEACHING YOUR CHILDREN TO BE KIND AND TO STAND UP FOR THEMSELVES

I have a dream that my four little children will one day live in a nation where they will not be judged by the color of their skin, but by the content of their character.
—Martin Luther King, Jr.

ONE OF THE MOST DIFFICULT challenges military children face is dealing with other children who are mean or unkind and often bully them on school buses, playgrounds, at afterschool programs, and in classrooms for various reasons. Military children experience several moments when their parents are gone so much that they start questioning why their parents deploy and why they move so much. They must also deal with moving to different communities and schools very frequently. They are often the new child on the block, in the school, in class, at the daycare center, or at after-school programs.

In our own home, when our two-year-old Meghan used to scratch my son, who was two years older than her, and he would come crying to us, we knew we had to do something, not only to help my daughter understand that it is not okay to hurt others but also for my son to stand up for himself and stop the scratching as much as he could before it even happened. As new and young parents then and also Christians, we attempted to raise our son to be a gentle soul and a faithful, polite boy. My son was naturally soft hearted and kind even though he was all boy, behavior wise. Our second daughter, however, was quite rough from the beginning. She was a sweet girl but fearless, tough, and a no-nonsense little mama. She was also mean to her older brother from what we saw. She scratched him repeatedly, stepped on his toes, and spat in his face sometimes when they were playing and something did not go right or when she did not have her way. This was a hard revelation, but it is the truth. A lot of these times, our son would come to us crying or telling us what his sister had done to him.

At the same time, we had reports that older children slapped our son and pushed him at different times at the afterschool care program that he attended in our new vicinity. My son would also let us know how other children were picking on him in class. At this point, it was clear that our son was a target of bullying at home from his younger sister and outside the home by other children. By this time, I had lost all my patience and we started aggressively teaching my son how to stand up for himself. We gave him the language to use and practical tactics to implement, including body positioning and walking away from situations that could lead to violent and mean behaviors when he was around other children. We took it one step at a time at home.

First, we explained to our daughter that she could not hurt others, no matter what. We then taught her what to do when she was upset. She could cry or scream out, she could walk away, or she could talk to us. She was quite young then, but we introduced deep breathing and the bear hug technique if she was extremely upset. We also went over the different feelings and let her know that she could get them out in different ways like coloring, drawing, talking, jumping, and praying. It was okay for her to cry, or even scream, as long as she was not doing that all day. We knew holding emotions in can be toxic now or later for anyone and we did not want her to feel like she needed to hold it all in.

It took tough love, time, patience, prayers, guidance, and practice to help my daughter to stop being mean to her brother. These days, when we think she is being bossy or mean to her younger sister, we catch it and talk with her, throwing more light on what she is expected to do instead. We have had positive compliments from her teachers and caregivers at daycare about how caring and helpful she is in school. We are happy that her mean phase is over and proud that she has transformed into a sweet girl.

I must say that this is a process and a skill that takes time to teach any child. It is hard to actually measure its success but when I hear our son telling his younger sibling to be nice and teaching her how to be kind, I smile. When we hear or see him stop a situation from escalating to mean behaviors, we commend him. We have seen so much progress in this area of his life and sometimes he will tell us what happens in school or afterschool care programs and how he stood up for himself or walked away from a situation or even stepped in to help another child who is the target of a bully.

Similarly, I have two friends who found themselves in comparable situations. My friend, Emily, has a daughter who is so sweet that other children take advantage of her kindness. The girl also worries that if she tells the other girls to their faces that she does not like their mean behavior, it will hurt their feelings, so she does nothing other than come home and tell her parents about all the mean comments and acts towards her from other children in her class.

In writing this chapter another friend of mine shared with me how she makes it a point to actually practice with her child often how to defend and protect herself.

So, what do you do when you find out that your well-trained child is unable to stand up for themselves when they need to?

First of all, you are going to have to see yourself as an assertive teacher, trainer, and coach in order to properly help your child learn and practice kindness as a value, and learning the skill of being assertive where they are not rude but actually standing up tall for themselves outside your door. Let's discuss other measures you can put in place.

STRATEGIES TO HELP YOUR CHILD STAND UP FOR THEMSELVES

Charity, they say, begins at home. If your child is going to be kind, assertive, confident, and positive, then home will play a major role in the molding and modeling process.

Here are a few pointers:

Let us start first with ourselves as the mom, dad, parent, aunty, or in whichever capacity we see ourselves and in whatever role we play in the child's life. Who are you? Are you kind to others? Are you bold and confident? Look at yourself in the mirror and answer that honestly. Let's dig a bit deeper. How did you learn to be kind, bold, and confident growing up? And now, how do you plan to model that in your home and to your own children?

How about standing up for yourself and speaking your mind, or giving your opinion? How bold are you and how often do you do that? I grew up learning to be the peacemaker in most situations and a lot of times did not bother to speak my mind. However, I have learned to express my opinion in a positive way in my personal and professional life. It took practice, time, and effort.

It is important to note that whatever we do in our home regarding this particular subject is shaping our children in one way or the other. Take an honest look at your home environment and answer a few questions for yourself. Do you have a democratic home where major decisions are made with everyone giving their opinions or do you live in an oppressed home or dictatorship home where only one person makes the decisions?

How do you handle conflict in the home environment as an adult? My children have seen me speak my mind in different situations, in tears when I am upset, in a calm manner, and also with an objective and strong opinion. I do not regret any of it because I want them to know and learn that I am not perfect. No home is perfect. What matters is that we are all allowed to be our true selves, especially in difficult situations. In the same way they have seen me happy, calm, respectful, polite, and gentle.

In my attempt to help the children I have worked with and with my own son I have used the following strategies:

Focused listening. I must be honest that this is hard for me on most days. I am usually exhausted by the end of the day. On days that I facilitate multiple training sessions plus one-on-one coaching sessions, I am truly spent by the end of the day. As an introvert, it means I am drained, and the slightest noise cracks me. My children obviously do not know and cannot understand this fully yet so when I pick them up from school or daycare, they start talking non- stop and actually sometimes whine and scream at the same time because they are tired, hungry, or had a long day in school, too. I have learned to develop a routine that can help me be there for them, even on days like that. If I am able to push in a thirty minute workout at the gym or just a walk before I pick them up, I am in a much better mood. Otherwise, I mostly just remain silent and listen with a nod when I am too tired to talk. I also play music for a few minutes when we all first get into the car to limit crying, yelling, and screaming as we drive home. I take a shower as soon as I get home. It gives me new energy to listen and focus on everything that they want to talk about that happened during their day. This way, I am in a better frame of mind to catch anything that needs to be addressed. Listening and, later on, following up together with your child is what will do the trick.

Assertive activities. I have found self-love and self-confidence challenge kits in the *Big Life Journal* very helpful. We set aside Saturday mornings when we are not rushing out for a basketball game or some other activity to work on these printable worksheets. Through these activities we talk about what makes us unique, why we love who we are, and what our bodies do for us. The last one we did together was on friendships. We did a positive and negative friendship relationship kit. Over a period of time, I could hear my son say, "I am not afraid I will lose my friends if I stand up for myself." And that was the point I had been meaning to send across for the longest time, especially if those friends were mean children.

Involving others. I remember storming into to the after school care program in my neighborhood one early morning when I had spent the previous night listening to my son tell me how the big boys slapped him and attempted to twist his head when they were waiting to be picked up from their school compound to go to the after-school care program. One of the staff had given me a report of the incident as protocol demanded, but I honestly did not get the gist of what really happened until my son told me. I needed to have a word with the director and to have an idea of the strategies he was putting in place to protect all the children in his care. We discussed strategies to help my son at home and he shared how his staff were going to be trained and supported so they could in turn be in a better position to supervise and protect all the children attending his program from bullying. We also discussed what consequences children who bully other children would receive. The director let me know that he spoke to the parents of those children and that they were suspended from the program for some days. It made me feel better as a parent that there were measures like that in place to protect the children in his program, including mine. Sometimes, involving other people and being consistent with the strategies to help your child stand up for themselves is what will do the trick.

Journaling. Use journaling as a reflective tool if your child can write, likes to draw, or enjoys painting on paper. Your goal is to help your child communicate feelings of doubt and self-critique, and to identify root causes of problems and evaluate any success as they try to be assertive. When my child journals, we spell out specific words in capital letters. We draw pictures of kindness, compassion, love, forgiveness, fearlessness, boldness and confidence. We also draw pictures of what is unacceptable by anyone, including them, as they learn and play with other children.

Practicing with your child. It is very common for children to feel nervous, intimidated, and uncomfortable about speaking up and communicating directly to other children who act mean toward them. The tool that will help your child get it all together is practicing assertive talk and self-defense strategies.

After you have listened and acknowledge your child's feelings, it is now time to practice what to say exactly to the other unkind child. You want to be respectful and kind, yet firm and clear at the same time.

These strategies take time to line up and for you to see results. Feel free to tweak them in a way that fits into your schedule and your own unique family dynamic and family lifestyle.

END OF CHAPTER REFLECTIVE QUESTIONS

What stories or experiences of bullying do you have to share?

_____

_____

_____

What strategies do you use to help your children be kind to others and stand up for themselves?

_____

_____

_____

What resources on bullying can you share with other parents that you know?

_____

_____

_____

CHAPTER TEN: DECIDING TO HOME SCHOOL OR PURSUE A CORPORATE CAREER

Children are like wet cement: whatever falls on them
makes an impression.
—Haim Ginott

ON MY OWN PARENTING JOURNEY, I have pursued a career outside of the home while raising our children as a military spouse more than I have been a full-time stay-at-home mom. I have homeschooled our children for only a short time at the time of writing this book. When we first started growing our family, we had thought of me being a stay-at-home mom full time and homeschooling our children, but we never fully decided it. This was pre-COVID. It was during PCS moves that I had the opportunity to homeschool my preschoolers for a short time. The experience gave me a taste of what that life on the other side can mean.

It was when the COVID-19 pandemic propelled most parents, including myself, to work from home and homeschool my children at the same time that gave me a different perspective on the subject. This experience of staying at home, schooling or supporting my children with virtual education not only opened my eyes but earned a deep respect for my friends who took a break from work and homeschooled their children for long periods of time.

My friend, Trisha, for example, homeschooled her twins for ten years, and I salute her. I personally think homeschooling is a personal choice, a divine calling, and a thoughtful family decision, a decision that can change along the way, as well.

In writing this book, I have interacted with parents who decided to retire from the military to be stay-at-home dads for a short time, further their education, and re-enter and start a civilian career. I have also met stay-at-home moms having enough of this homeschooling thing and finally deciding to go back to the workforce in order to build a career for themselves. In Maureen's own words, "It was just not working for me and my son anymore, so we both agreed that he should go to school, and I should take a break." I met Maureen, who had been homeschooling her children for eight years, at a women's Bible study group during one vacation Bible study that our children attended.

In my interaction with both fulltime stay-at home parents and parents who are crushing corporate career goals, together with my own experiences having seen both sides of the coin, none of the journeys are smooth. In most cases, both sets of parents are filled with guilt or think they are missing out and not doing enough. For example, full time stay-at home parents feel guilty not supporting the home with a paycheck and think they are missing out on the business and corporate life. Some think they have achieved less compared to their counterparts who go to work every day outside the home. At the same time, parents who pursue a career out of the home feel the same heat of guilt for not making enough time to be with their children. Some of my friends in this category choke themselves with shame when their children pick up certain behaviors and they think the behavior is a result of their children being exposed to other negative behaviors exhibited by other children in schools or daycare centers. In effect, each party feels overwhelmed, tired, and sometimes lost. Neither choice in my opinion is perfect or glamorous.

Sometimes my husband is gone seven to ten months out of the twelve months in a calendar year for several years throughout his career when he is on sea duty. At the time of writing this book, I am also raising three young children under the age of ten, so I must be both mom and dad at the same time. And finally, I am pursuing a career out of the home, so I am stretched thin a good number of days as I juggle all my responsibilities. A good number of military spouses are in this category.

So here I am, wide awake at nearly one in the morning in my Atago Hills duplex bedroom in Iwakuni. My children are fast asleep. My husband is miles away on the Island of Guam, and I am up having a real talk with myself in my journal answering tough questions like, *What is really important to me in my career right now? What do I really want and how do I make my family a priority whiles pursuing my dreams at the same time?*

I am taking the time to think and brainstorm so I can decide what is best for my family and also for myself as a person. I came up with three words to sum up what I think is really critical to me as a parent and military working spouse at this stage of our family life and how to make it happen:

FAMILY. FUN. FINANCE.

First, I need a flexible schedule that will allow me to get the little human beings ready for the day and one that I can be right there when my children get of school by two or three o'clock. My son has basketball practice and my daughters have ballet classes and swimming lessons. Plus, I want to feed them homecooked meals to nourish their bodies and souls as part of growing them.

Yes. I know, most parents who pursue careers outside the home give up on all of these because let's just face it and be real: today's work demands anything and everything from you. You literally do not have the time or the energy for most of these things. To make things worse, you are torn between achieving your career goals or beating yourself up as a parent because you are unable to help your child the way you really want to. The guilt from giving them the tablets or asking them to watch TV so they can leave you alone because you are exhausted from work can eat you up. I chanced upon a saying on social media that read *society expects parents to raise children like they do not work and to work as if they are not raising children*. How true.

But honestly, I think if you can sit down with a piece of paper and start brainstorming on a few things, you can come up with how to really crush your corporate goals and still be the parent who can support your children in different ways to grow their talents. In your brainstorming session, identify what resources and help that you can get from other family members, friends, and in your community.

Second, I want to have *fun* in pursuing a career or in what I do for work. It is only by doing so that I am not coming home stressed and cranky and finding myself screaming and yelling at the innocent children who look at me like *I think Mommy is going crazy and we don't know why*. So, on this second piece I clearly wrote that I find joy and fulfilment when I work towards being a thought leader in my career. I have gained experience, gathered certificates, and am currently garnishing my expertise. At this point, I am attracted to writing, training, coaching, consulting, and mentoring individuals to succeed in their careers and supporting organizations to grow, expand, and thrive. I will focus on training through speaking engagements and publications. Done. Will it be fun? We will see. And truth be told, I have been positioning myself purposely for some time now. I would turn down some positions or not apply for them at all, not because I do not qualify for them but just because that is not my focus or ultimate goal in the long run.

Lastly, I need my career to reward me financially so I can take care of my family's immediate needs and wants as well as invest in their future. For example, I want to be able to afford a decent home for my family, food, clothing, and give them travel experiences in the form of family vacations. Most importantly, I want to be in the position where I can support my children's future by helping them pay for a college education and invest in their business ventures. For myself, I want to be able to save and invest toward my own retirement. I understand that my husband is the breadwinner and respect him as the head of the family, but I am also my own person and need to bring my part to the table for our family.

In conclusion, deciding to either homeschool or pursue a career outside the home while parenting is totally up to you. Each choice has its own ups and downs and real lessons to learn from and opportunities to grow. Praying for wisdom and guidance, having a winning attitude, setting a goal for yourself, and having a strong support system is what will help you succeed whichever path you decide to tread.

FACTORS TO CONSIDER WHEN CHOOSING TO BE A FULL-TIME STAY-AT-HOME PARENT

1. Time. The first thing to consider is how long you want or choose to be a full-time stay-at-home parent. Would you be doing this until your children go to high school, college, or just during their early, formative years?

2. Educational Resources. Since you would be teaching your children how to read, spell, and write, think through where you would go for resources, either from books or online or information from people you know you can trust.

3. Support. How do you plan to support the social and emotional development of your children? Your children will still need friends to play with. Since you and your children may not be seeing a lot of people, do you plan to coordinate or look for playdates? How involved would you be?

4. Your personal goals or interests. You are still a person with potential, talent, interests, and skills. How would you still be able to do those things that matter to you and who you want to be when the children leave your nest?

5. Do you plan to start a home business? I have a few friends who are full-time stay-at-home moms who also sell online products or have a small business idea or goal they are pursuing.

6. Budgeting. Since it may mainly be one income supporting expenses, how do you plan to stick to a balanced budget? Reaching out to other parents who are experienced in doing this could be helpful. In addition to this, many installations have budgeting classes for military families that can arm you with the right information and tools to make it work.

FACTORS TO CONSIDER WHEN PURSUING A FULL-TIME CAREER OUTSIDE THE HOME

1. The first thing to consider is the career field and whether you want to work full-time, part-time, or continue your military service (if you are both in the service), and for how long you want to work. I spoke to a few friends whiles writing this book. One friend shared with me that she joined the military later on when her spouse was already deep in it. She had taken the early years to support the upbringing and the education of her children. When she felt comfortable, she then decided to join the military just like her husband. My other friend and her husband started as dual military. However, she decided to retire early from the service so one parent would be home to take care of the children. I also interacted with my friend Kate, who is a dentist with the US Navy. Both she and her husband have been dual military service members since day one. They have been serving and raising their two children beautifully.

2. Schedule. How flexible can your work schedule be? If your children attend daycare you still need to be able to drop them and pick them up before and after work, for example.

3. Your support system. Who are the people you can count on to help you when you are stuck at work and your spouse is deployed or unable to get out of work?

4. Telework. Consider working remotely or from home if you are able to. COVID-19 has driven most companies and organizations to maximize teleworking options for their employees. If this option is easier and better for you because you have to raise your children and support them with virtual schooling, go for it or search for telework positions.

5. Balance. How do you plan to balance work and family? A strong balance between work and family life is critical to your own wellbeing, your relationships, your family, and your home. Since your spouse will be deployed a lot, finding simple ways to add balance to your lifestyle will help your family thrive. For example, take a few days off and do fun things with your children. Travel when and where you can go, experience things, visit local parks, or sometimes just rest at home and do fun things with them.

END OF CHAPTER REFLECTIVE QUESTIONS

What do you like best about your current situation as a full time stay-at home parent or a parent who is pursuing a career full-time, or as dual military parents?

_____

_____

_____

What strategies could you implement to ensure you have a work and family life balance?

_____

_____

_____

Share your experience working from home and supporting your children with virtual school at the same time during COVID-19.

_____

_____

_____

CHAPTER ELEVEN: CREATING YOUR VILLAGE OF PARENTS

There can be no keener revelation of society's soul than the way in which it treats its children.
—Nelson Mandela

JOURNALING IS ONE OF MY hobbies and this morning I wrote down a few powerful words during my quiet time:

My Family. My Life. My All.

I had always known that but today was a different feeling, encompassing new thoughts and dreams. At this moment, I find myself in a petite Japanese hotel in the city of Osaka as I wait to catch my flight to Guam to meet my husband, who is on a short detachment. I am traveling alone. I have not traveled to a different country all by myself since I started having children. My three children are seven, five, and three years old at the time of writing this chapter. At this same period too, my family and I are living in Iwakuni. This is our second tour in Japan but our first time in Iwakuni. It is a little bit different from the other places that we have lived in Japan. My husband's deployment year usually begins with short detachments then the long deployment. It is my first time meeting him on a short detachment in Guam. I smile at the thought. It will be a mini-vacation and an anniversary celebration in the midst of work and other things that we have planned to do. I am going without my children. I can finally breathe for a minute.

I left Iwakuni in the evening as I had to catch a train to a different city to board my flight the following morning. Last night, as I dragged my luggage onto the *shinkansen* to the airport, it literally dawned on me that a huge part of me was missing my children, even though at first, I had thought that leaving them was great opportunity to spend quality time with my husband. I fought hard to hold my tears. I could not believe how much I was missing my children already. I was only going to be gone for three days. Suddenly, all the times they drove me crazy did not matter at all anymore nor did the tough moments where I felt like pulling my hair out and leaving to be alone.

I also wrote down clearly and exactly what I wanted when it comes to the kind of family I wanted to grow, nurture, and release into the world. Our world. These were the other powerful statements of prophecy that I penned in purple ink in my blue journal:

I want to create a home where each individual person, including myself, thrives and becomes the best version of themselves.

First things first. I want to raise children who will grow up and fear God. Children who are:

Happy. Confident. Responsible. Respectful. Honest. Kind. Helpful. Daring enough to chart their own course without permission. Children who will succeed in their personal and professional lives.

As I closed the cap of the pen, I knew that there was no way I could do this all on my own. No one can. Really. No matter how confident, educated, or rich you are. *Some things are just not meant to be done alone,* in my opinion and experience.

First, I knew that I am going to need grace, wisdom, and strength from above. In addition to that, I am also going to need great health, a certain mindset, a career that will allow me a flexible schedule, a fulfilling purpose and one that is also financially rewarding to support my family. But that is not all at all. I am going to need to learn to understand children, parenting, and taking care of myself so I can be fit spiritually, mentally, emotionally, and physically to nurture young minds in our home and life.

Above all, I am going to need a *village* to raise my children. A village of other people to include my blood family relatives—my mother, my in-laws, my siblings, my church family, my God-given friends, and those who I consider as a military family, and teachers in communities we live in. Think of it. Everyone is going to have a share a little piece in your child's life—intentionally and unintentionally. Everyone is going to play a role in molding and forming your child in a different fashion.

Intentionally creating your village that can help you as you raise your child and support them to thrive is the takeaway from this chapter.

HOW TO CREATE YOUR OWN VILLAGE OF PARENTS

Creating your village of parents is a personal choice but a necessity, especially for military families who are often far away from family. It is also a process that sometimes comes naturally but takes time. It takes time to get to know people and to form relationships with others in order to feel comfortable for them to be part of your family. In our own experience, we have seen many people joining us on our journey to raise our children in one way or the other. Family, trusted friends in our new installations, childcare professionals at the daycare that they attend, teachers at their schools, Sunday school teachers in our local churches, and coaches at sports and dance clubs who teach, cheer, and motivate our children to believe in themselves. As much as these categories of people are not parents of our children, they play a major role in our children's development.

Key factors to consider when you are building your village of parents is making sure that those people you choose have the same values that you have and that you have a common understanding of what discipline looks like. Another important thing to do is to arm your children with information on how to say no when anyone touches them inappropriately. Here are more some tips and strategies to consider when creating your own village of parents.

1. Prayerfully choose your village of parents. I am that person who can be overprotective when it comes to the people I allow into our life, home, and my family.

2. Trust the process of parenting, raising, and supporting your little ones. The different people all play their part whether we admit or not.

3. Be a part of the village that supports other parents. As military families, whether we like it or not, we are often far away from home and sometimes in unknown corners around the world. Making yourself available to support other parents is a call for us all.

4. Be involved with your child's activities at school. Participate in parent-teacher family conferences so you can discuss how your child is doing in school and what you want the teachers to work on with them.

5. Let your children understand that other people who fall under the category of village of parents may be taking part in their lives and playing major roles, but you are their parents at the end of the day.

END OF CHAPTER REFLECTIVE QUESTIONS

What is your take on the popular saying that *it takes a village to raise a child*?

_____

_____

_____

What roles have others played in your own child's life in school, church, or community that you have been proud of?

_____

_____

_____

What strategies have you used or are you using to build your village of parents?

_____

_____

_____

CHAPTER TWELVE: GUIDING POSITIVE BEHAVIOR

In my world, there are no bad kids, just impressionable conflicted young people wrestling with emotions and impulses, trying to communicate their feelings and needs the only way they know how.
—Janet Lansbury

THE FIRST POSITION I HELD when I first moved overseas was working with school-age children between the ages of five and twelve in our school-age care program as a programs assistant and later on moved up as programs assistant leader to a cluster of preschool classrooms at the Child Development Center on base where we were stationed at the time. Our preschool program was a multi-aged preschool with children who were between the ages of three and five.

I love working with children, so the position was an answered prayer but also one that gave me a run for my money because of the challenging behaviors of the children in the classrooms that I supervised. I was leading a group of refined childcare professionals who did all they could to keep a smooth-running classroom, but some days things were just too hard and uncontrollable due to challenging behaviors the children in our care exhibited. When I started having my own children, I had a firsthand experience of some of these same challenging behaviors in my own home some days. This led me to start looking deeply and researching more about guiding positive behaviors in children, first for myself at home, and second for my position at work and for the larger community.

Positive behavior is expected by adults, parents, or teachers. These are behaviors that contribute to a safe, peaceful, and conducive home or classroom environment. When the opposite happens, we typically say the child is exhibiting challenging or negative behaviors. Some of the challenging behaviors that I have experienced working with children include: failure to follow simple directions, headbanging, throwing themselves on the floor, running away, throwing things at other children or adults, spitting, hitting other children or adults, screaming, crying non-stop, hurting others with no remorse, yelling, using inappropriate language, and refusing to participate in group activities or do schoolwork.

Children usually exhibit negative behaviors at different stages of their development as well as through some periods of their life for various reasons. Your child is not immune from showing behaviors that are uncalled for, like biting, hitting you and others around them, screaming, yelling, throwing tantrums, spiting at you or others, escaping, rebelling, not following directions or simple instructions, and saying mean words to you and others, just to name a few examples.

However, understanding the underlying causes, maintaining your cool, and arming yourself with the right information and the tools and techniques to respond to the specific behavior is what will get you through. In some cases, you may need a medical evaluation or to reach out to external resources, including behavior specialists to assist you as well. If you are a Christian, lifting up your child in prayer and praying for wisdom, strength, and guidance for yourself will be your first move. It is key to remember not to think of your child as a *bad* child or label them with specific names that associate with the behavior that they are portraying. You should also not call them evil or little devils. Your aim is to help your child limit the unacceptable and unsafe behavior and not to target your child as evil or bad luck. Children are precious gifts from above and must be called and treated a such.

TAKE A S.E.A.T AND LET'S DISCUSS WHY CHILDREN BEHAVE THE WAY THEY DO SOMETIMES

S.E.A.T is an acronym meaning *sensory, escape, attention,* and *tangibles* used in the study of the four functions of behavior by Board Certified Behavior Analysts (BCBAs) to understand why a specific challenging behavior occurs and how to respond to that behavior. Almost all children's behavior is a form of communication.

According to the Functions of Behavior theory, children exhibit negative behaviors when they have a sensory need, want to escape an activity, desire your attention, and/or want a tangible item. Let's delve a little deeper on this one.

Say your four-year-old child, Maud, finds pleasure in playing with soap all the time. When you enter the bathroom to take a quick shower, she goes to the kitchen and pours the liquid laundry detergent on the floor and rubs all over. She enjoys the smell, finds pleasure in how it feels and sees nothing wrong with seeing it all over the floor. When you get out of the shower, you call out her name, but she does not respond and immediately you know something is wrong. You rush downstairs and your heart leaps, and your voice goes up. You have warned her several times, but she does not seem to get it. Maud is satisfying her own *sensory* need and curiosity.

Your best friend calls you and laments how her fifteen-year-old son, Jason, is having issues at school. His grades are falling and his tutors always call her when he misses some classes even though he is in school. He does this all the time no matter how much she talks to him before dropping him off at school. Jason finds comfort as he *escapes* the classes, so his parents are having to deal with this all the time.

As you get ready to go to the grocery store with Maud, you ask her to hold the grocery list. You two have a jolly ride to the store. At the store, she wants a chocolate candy, but that is not on the list and you would rather use that money for wipes for the new baby. You are on maternity leave with no pay, so you are on tight budget. Maud screams and throws herself on the floor. She wants a *tangible* item. This behavior is for physical items like candy or toys.

Getting home, the baby starts crying and immediately you know it is time to feed her. Maud wants you to play a game with her. You explain that you will play with her as soon as you get done feeding the baby, but Maud is not having it. She kicks and throws toys across the room. Maud is acting out for your *attention.* On the other hand, she may be hungry, tired, or sleepy herself.

Each of these scenarios give you an idea of some of the challenges you might have experienced with your own children. Knowing what to expect and using different tools and techniques can help you work with your child to minimize the behavior. In some cases, you will have to use or provide special tools (such as sensory boxes filled with tactile items), employ breathing techniques, sign up for therapy sessions, create visual charts, or use social stories to create rules with the children plus be consistent with a gentle, firm approach to redirect the behavior.

UNIQUE CHALLENGES FACING MILITARY CHILDREN

Military children face unique challenges, including long deployments, frequent moves, and have parents who are sometimes highly stressed with their jobs. In my own experience and in my work experience with other military children, the root causes of most behaviors are due to frequent deployments when the children miss their parents and are not having it. Typically, two weeks before a parent deploys, we see a huge rise in negative behaviors in the childcare center where I work. We experience similar behavior around two weeks before the deployed parent comes home.

In the same way, during Permanent Change of Duty Station (PCS) moves children feel anxious as parents go through a variety of emotions as well. Even when families arrive at their new stations, they are normally compelled to live in temporary lodging until they are assigned a home. When this happens, families are forced to live in suitcases until household goods arrive. This situation can trigger negative behaviors. Eventually, the children adjust and start living normally again.

Another underlying factor for why children show challenging behaviors is the environment at home. If a child is being raised in a negative or abusive home environment, they usually portray it. When parents are going through a difficult divorce or separation, the children show it as well in the form of negative behaviors.

In your home, even room temperature can affect very young children. If the room is too hot, they might feel uncomfortable and agitated and cry a lot. A disorganized and chaotic home can affect behavior in certain cases, too, as can the kind of food you feed your children. High levels of sugars and unhealthy snacking or eating makes some children hyper and overreact.

OTHER TECHNIQUES TO GUIDE POSITIVE BEHAVIOR

1. Breathe. Relax and keep your cool when children are acting out, especially for your attention. Personally, I become very quiet, especially when it is an overwhelming situation that involves screaming, yelling, or crying consistently. I also practice deep breathing and count to ten before I respond. That way, I do not end up yelling or screaming myself and complicating matters.

2. Digging into the root cause of the behavior or what triggers the behavior can be helpful information that can allow you to be on your guard and help you limit the occurrence of the situation in the future. As a military family, if the root cause of the specific challenging behavior is a long deployment, I take time to explain to my child that Daddy will be home soon. We also color, draw pictures, and write letters to send Daddy. Recently, one strategy I used was to have my daughter keep a photo of her and her Dad under her pillow when she was extremely upset one evening and started screaming and crying non-stop.

3. Guide and discipline in love. A lot of times, children go through emotions that they do not understand or have the words to even explain. They show or communicate this in their unacceptable behaviors. Guiding the child by developing classroom or home rules together, talking about acceptable and unacceptable behaviors, and showing them the consequences of their behavior can help the situation.

4. Be firm yet gentle. Children are very smart, especially the ones that exhibit challenging and negative behaviors. They know which buttons to push and how to feed off of your mood and reaction. Being very firm with the rules developed

together while being gentle at the same time is what some children need. My advice would be to use your gentle, firm tone of voice when you have to.

5. Seek help and ask for medical evaluation. Trust me, some behaviors may have a medical origin. It is prudent to talk to your child's pediatrician if you are concerned about some of the challenging behaviors that your child shows. There might be some diagnosis and treatment or support for your child that you may not be aware of.

6. Talk to others. My friend reached out to her mom when she was unsure what was happening and if the behavior of her son was normal for that stage or not. She found that getting insight into how to handle the behavior and support her son was helpful. Again, another friend reached out to another parent who has children of the same age and just sharing ideas on what strategies has worked or not was something he found useful. Some childcare programs, like the Marine Corps Child and Youth Programs, have a behavior specialist who is trained to support children with challenging behaviors. Reaching out to a behavior specialist is a huge resource as well. In addition, the Military Family Life Consultants (MFLCs) are on every military base and they work with children and families. Speaking to them can give you insight into supporting your child. They are able to work with your children in schools, after school care programs, child development centers and can also meet you and your family if you want to talk to them.

7. Take another look at your home environment. The atmosphere can play a major role in how children behave. If your home environment is constantly cluttered, dirty, or there is tension in your home, it can affect the behavior of your children. Strive to keep your home setting decluttered, clean, peaceful, and calm as much as you can.

8. Provide sensory kits. Children like to play with different toys and learn with different materials of different textures. You can put together a simple sensory bin by purchasing simple fidgeting toys, playdough, kinetic sand, different textured balls and colorful liquid tubes that you can use with your children. These sensory bins are also popular in most classroom environments as well.

9. Use social stories. Creating simple, short, and personalized stories that connect with the child can be a helpful strategy in trying to explain events, consequences, expectations, and behaviors for children. You can create social stories on themes like, *How I can use my words, Listening is a cool thing, I can get ready for school in the morning,* or *Me and my mommy,* just to mention a few.

10. Adjust your routines to include more family time and creating memories. Building a positive relationship and a bond with your children is at the heart of guiding positive behavior. In addition to working around your home environment, readjusting your family routines to include quality family time and creating memories and enjoying experiences together can help limit certain unacceptable behaviors at home, in school or at daycare centers.

11. Use positive reinforcement, distraction, and a reward system to track progress. As a parent, affirming your child and using a reward system when they make an attempt to listen or follow instructions can be helpful. In the case of small children, you can distract them with another activity.

12. For older children, show them love by spending more time with them. Listen to them. Connect with them and help them understand and trust you as the parent whose role is to guide and support them to succeed in school and life by taking small steps.

END OF CHAPTER REFLECTIVE QUESTIONS

What is your definition of acceptable or positive behavior in your own home or classroom, if you are a teacher?

_____

_____

_____

Share your experience dealing with children with difficult behaviors.

_____

_____

_____

What strategies have you used, or do you currently use to guide positive behavior that has really worked very well for you?

_____

_____

_____

CHAPTER THIRTEEN: ADDRESSING PROBLEMATIC SEXUAL BEHAVIORS IN CHILDREN

Children must be taught how to think, not what to think.
—Margaret Mead

TALK TO MY CHILDREN ABOUT *sex*? That is difficult, I will blatantly admit.

This is why:

First of all, I am Christian. We do not talk about sex at Sunday school.

Second, I was born and raised in Ghana, plus I am the old-school type of mom, even though I consider myself young. If you do not know, now you know that it is a taboo in most cultures in Africa to talk about sex, at least the part that I come from and especially when I was growing up.

But I remember preaching on air when I was growing as a child rights advocate and radio journalist about the importance of sex education. My favorite phrase was *if you fail to talk to your children about sex, someone else will do it for you in the wrong way at the wrong time and it may be too late*. That is and was absolutely true, but here I am as an adult finding it very uncomfortable to talk about it to my own children, especially when they ask questions like, "Mommy how did we come out of your belly?"

I have talked to my children about how each of them was housed in my belly for nine months. They love the stories and I tell them which ones did kickboxing in my belly, who was sticking their feet out the most, who must have been dancing *shaka zulu* in my belly, and who was found sucking their thumb during the ultrasound, as well as who was the shiest among them when we were trying to identify their gender. That is where the stories ended, for the most part. But, how on earth do I phrase how I pushed each of them out of my vagina?

You see, I can admit that it isn't easy to now have to put my money where my mouth is. From experience, it was an easy game to criticize and lambast adults and leaders when they fail us as young people than being that adult or leader, ready to stick your head out and hold the standard high for society.

Today, the tables have turned. It is my turn to sit still, get in line, keep calm and learn how to address sexual issues as part of raising my children.

WHAT PROBLEMATIC SEXUAL BEHAVIORS IN CHILDREN

The first time I really paid attention to the topic was at work. As a training and curriculum specialist working with childcare professionals, one of my key responsibilities is to coordinate subject matter expert trainings. These are stake holders and professionals who have wide experience and deep knowledge on certain topics and who come to our centers and break it down for us when it has to do with certain subjects. It was during one of those trainings that I really paid attention to problematic sexual behaviors in children starting as young as three.

I remember sitting still and keeping my eyes glued to the presentation on addressing sexual behaviors in children, ready to learn from this expert, Miss Doreen. She was a professional and an expert that I admired and respected. She was very knowledgeable and has a sweet spirit. She was very friendly and witty, too and used several personal experiences to connect with us.

As she went through the slides, the presentation was loaded with new information, statics, and a picture of how things may look like for each person. Let us call it perspective. It was a reminder and a confident approach to me.

The key point is to learn to get comfortable in addressing sexual behaviors in your children. Basically, learn to talk to your children about sex. The point is, whether we like it or not, whether we are comfortable or not, whether we are old school, new school, or no school at all, we've got to learn the ropes of the game. Learning the terms and adopting new strategies to address sexual behaviors is a very important piece in growing your children in this modern era.

As a matter of fact, in researching further and writing about this topic, the revelations and stories from different professionals and families were eye-opening, especially in defining what is considered normal and problematic when it comes to sexual behaviors in children. Typically, children between the ages of five and eight are beginning to be aware of their own private parts. At this stage, they are also curious about life cycles and want to know how babies are made and or where babies come from, for example. You may see them touch or explore their private parts occasionally, playfully discuss private parts with peers or ask them to do the same and may even initiate or participate in pretend play involving being the mommy or daddy caring for a baby or a doctor checking a sick child.

In the same way, children between the ages of six and twelve begin to demand privacy, show knowledge of sexuality, physical changes, and reproduction. It is common for children of this age to develop pubic hair, and the girls may grow breasts or start menstruation. Children at this age may also develop attractions to peers and may also use foul language to tell inappropriate stories or jokes. All of these are considered normal.

However, the sexual behaviors in developing children and youth that are considered problematic are defined by the Department of Defense (DoD) as "those behaviors initiated by children and youth under the age of eighteen that involve sexual body parts (genitals, anus, buttocks, or breasts) in a manner that deviates from normative or typical sexual behavior and are developmentally inappropriate and/or potentially harmful to the individual initiating the behavior or others."

To throw more light on this, sexual behaviors that are considered problematic depend on the age of the child, how frequent the behavior occurs, and the consequences of the behaviors.

CAUSES OF PROBLEMATIC SEXUAL BEHAVIORS AMONG CHILDREN

The first cause of problematic sexual behaviors in children is a history of sexual abuse because children who are victims themselves may show signs of problematic sexual behaviors.

The second cause of problematic sexual behaviors in children and youth is attributed to the media. Children who are exposed to highly sexualized media with little or no supervision from adults tend to indulge in inappropriate sexual behaviors.

In addition, family violence, specifically physical violence between adults in the home can put children at risk of problematic sexual behaviors, as does child neglect.

It is important to learn how to respond to sexual behaviors and know when to seek help for your child. It is very important to maintain your calm so you can gather your thoughts and redirect the behavior if you catch it in the moment. In addition, it is crucial to listen and address it by teaching what is appropriate through discussions if you happen to learn about the behavior after the fact. It is always a good idea to speak to your child's doctor or behavior specialists if you are unsure if a specific sexual behavior is normal or problematic.

CALLING IT WHAT IT IS

A penis is a penis. A vagina is a vagina. Period. In the same way, buttocks are buttocks and breasts are breasts. It is essential to teach the children to identify those private parts and learn to call them their real names and nothing else. Trust me, I am very guilty of this. I used to shy away from the real names and would call buttocks *concon* or *bambam* when I talked to my children. It is my field of work that shifted that mindset and terminology. If children are not able to identify those parts and call them as they are and someone molests for them, for example, and they are not able to say their real names, that person could walk away free. We pray it never happens, but you also don't want that person to walk away because you never taught your children to call them by their exact names.

When it comes to talking to children about sex itself, I say gauge the age, so you know what to say exactly. Start with an easy conversation. Let it be part of your usual conversation from time to time so you check in with your child to know what they know and what they may be picking up from the media or their peers.

Finally, arm your children with the right kind of information on the subject. Start with buying simple books on sex, reproductive health, and procreation. Read together and discuss it. This will open the door to other conversations. You will be able to see many other teachable moments as well.

END OF CHAPTER REFLECTIVE QUESTIONS

What is your experience talking about sex with your children or your parents growing up?

_____

_____

_____

Have you worked with a child who exhibited problematic sexual behaviors before? How did you spot the problem and what did you do?

_____

_____

_____

Share your list of all the places to find help, resources, and information to address problematic sexual behaviors.

_____

_____

_____

CHAPTER FOURTEEN: COPING IN EMERGENCY SITUATIONS AS A FAMILY

Children are great imitators, so give them
something great to imitate.
—Anonymous

#COVID-19 pandemic. It was Friday, March 13, 2020. I will always remember that it was the day the United States government declared a national health emergency due to the rapid spreading of the novel coronavirus known COVID-19. At the same time, the World Health Organization confirmed that the virus is a worldwide pandemic. Everywhere on the news there was something corona-related. The tsunami of cases was overwhelming and scary. Every hour, the news reported that the virus had made its way to new countries and continents like a lightning strike.

As I wrote down these words in my Hilton hotel room in Guam, I was filled with mixed feelings: fear, anger, frustration, disappointment—but also a little bit of hope. I feared for my children I had left behind for a couple of days to visit my husband who was on a short detachment to Guam. Would they shut down or ban travel? What if I got stuck here? What if my children caught the virus whiles I was here? So many *what ifs.*

My phone beeped and I checked. It was my supervisor.

Roll calling Pearl. Respond ASAP and let me know if there are any travel plan changes.

I could tell something was wrong. The situation was getting worse worldwide. Our president had just spoken. The various military bases in Japan, including the base where we are stationed are taking vigorous precautions. I texted to confirm with my supervisor that my flight back to Iwakuni was still on as scheduled. My heart sank for a minute as I waited for her response back.

Her response was easy and simple to understand: *Heads up, you have a 14-day self-quarantine when you get back.*

What does this self-quarantine even entail? The question slipped uninvited into my thoughts as I stared at the phone for a moment. *Okay, does my 14-day self-quarantine start when I departed or when I return?* I typed.

Upon arrival, she responded with a short answer.

Got it was my response as I stood there clueless, asking myself what this whole corona thing is all about? For a moment I could not wrap my head around what was going on.

For the next couple of days, I kept glued to the news as I managed to enjoy the sights and sand of the Island. I am not much fan of television, but I checked CNN on my phone to stay abreast with what was going on. I also checked updates from the commanding officer of the base I was returning to. He posted updates frequently to keep us informed. You can imagine my anxiety and uneasiness for the days that followed. To be honest, I could not wait to get back home.

At that moment, I actually wished I had my children with us. Just in case the worst happened, I would not want to be separated from my children on two different continents.

My flight back to Japan was only three hours and forty minutes. The entire time I was in the middle of somewhere in the skies I prayed. I prayed for a cure, a vaccination, total healing, and, most importantly, a safe flight to get back home and to my children. I just knew that everything could be worked out if I got home and stayed with my children. My husband was scheduled be home a couple of weeks after my arrival.

When I finally got home it was close to midnight, but I was glad I made it eventually. I had the option to sleep in the city of Osaka before proceeding to our home in Iwakuni in the morning, but at that point all I wanted to do was just to get home and deal with whatever was at stake. Upon entering my home, I heaved a big sigh of relief. The house was empty, of course. My children were with my neighbor, and I had just left my husband back in Guam. I had six hours to sleep and then go get my children. One thing was for sure: I was not letting my children go anywhere. No school or daycare. I just wanted to hug them and snuggle with them all day in the midst of the virus. I was excited when I saw my children in the morning, and they were also very happy to see me.

Life from then on was quite different. My self-quarantine began immediately. They used different terms on our base for instance restriction of movement (ROM) or self-quarantine. They both seemed to mean the same thing. Honestly, I was too tired and wanted to be with my children, so it did not really matter. I was going to be in my happy place—home with my children who I had missed a lot. I followed the base directive and got screened at the branch health clinic on base and returned to my home to resume my self-quarantine.

Being asked to stay home to reduce the spread of the virus if I had it potentially meant a slightly different kind of life. At first, it made sense and then later it did not make sense to me. At first, it seemed easy, but later on it was hard staying home and not being able to go out.

It was more of a psychological thing to go through. The anxiety, panic attacks, stress of knowing and not knowing, understanding and not understanding were more sickening than anything.

I can say that it was hard for me to explain our new normal to our children. For example, it was difficult for me to make them understand why they could not go out and play anymore for the next fourteen days because we had to self-quarantine for the first time in our lives. I also had to find a way to explain to our children why they could not touch or hug children they had just seen the day before because now they had come into direct contact with me, who just travelled. And finally, I had let them know that I could not take them to their favorite restaurant, Hamazushi, to eat sushi.

From here on, I knew I had to change my way of thinking, increase my level of positivity, and get it moving. I had to look deep within myself to find gratitude. I was grateful that I was going to be spending time with my children drawing and eating breakfast in our pajamas. I also decided to use this time to clean, organize, and sanitize our home. Most importantly, I planned to use this time to finish writing this book. It helped once I could have a possible daily routine with the children being at home, setting goals, and making time for self-care, as well as connecting with others. During this time, I learned that touch, human connection, physical hugs, and smiles are priceless.

QUARANTINE AND VIRTUAL SCHOOL DURING THE PANDEMIC

Seven days into our self-quarantine, my husband arrived from Guam and we had to quarantine as a family, meaning we would be in isolation for twenty-one days total. We had the option to quarantine him in a separate room within the house but in all honesty, it was not feasible.

The children had missed their dad for some time and we just could not see how they would not touch or cuddle with their father living under the same room for two weeks. Our community was very supportive. My friends offered to go on grocery runs for us. My colleague, Flavia, brought the children different games, books, and toys from the improvised *corona* store that the base came up with. We were able to give a permission note to my friend, Alithea, to pick up our mail from the post office during our restriction of movement (ROM).

As a family, we did not have much routine for the first time. We slept and woke up late for the first few days. We cooked and ate great meals. We also played, listened to music, and incorporated exercise using Youtube videos. We called our friends and families using video chats. Some days we enjoyed it. Other days we felt very bored and missed everyone and everything we used to do. In short, some days went well and the other days we were all just cranky and nothing seemed to work at all. During those times we would try to watch a movie or just retire to bed and sleep it away.

Just when we were somehow getting used to our new normal in our own home, we received the news that the Department of Defense Education was transitioning into virtual school for the remainder of the school year. At the time, my son was the only one in school and was wrapping up second grade. Virtual schooling meant computers, more screen time, and being available to make sure that he was supported in the virtual classroom. The first few days were both exciting but overwhelming for us as we navigated through the technology and online school routine and class schedules. There were different websites, login information, and emails to consume from the school and teachers. Working fulltime outside the house after the quarantine period and supporting my son with virtual school at the same time was also very challenging for us.

GOING THROUGH DEPLOYMENT DURING THE PANDEMIC

Just a few weeks after we got out of quarantine and wrapped up virtual school for the academic year, my husband was scheduled to deploy. Preparation for deployment in the midst of the coronavirus was at a different level. As part of COVID-19 pre-deployment preparation and safety measures, my husband and the other sailors aboard the base that were scheduled to deploy had to go through a separate quarantine before moving to the ship. This means my husband was leaving about two to three weeks earlier to quarantine first before flying to the ship for deployment.

In addition to this new quarantine procedure, we did not get to see the usual deployment break that we typically get because of the virus. We also could not travel as much as we had planned. To survive through this, the children and I got busy with our garden project, enjoyed summer camp on the base, attended child and youth programs and visited local places when we were allowed to.

COPING STRATEGIES DURING EMERGENCY SITUATIONS

In emergency situations I have found the following strategies helpful, especially with children.

1. Explain to children what is going on exactly in terms they can easily understand and without jargon. I explained to the children about the virus and what we needed to do to avoid getting into contact with it. I also explained the need to be mindful of how we used hand soaps and toilet rolls, for example, so we did not run out of them.

2. Assure your children that you still love them, that you are stronger together as a family, and remind them that everything will be okay in the end. Preach the famous saying that *this too shall pass.*

3. Give children an idea what it means for them, like more time at home, using time wisely, not wasting food, etc.

4. Have an emergency plan or evacuation plan to include emergency bags and non-perishable food supplies.

5. Set a goal. In this case, my goal was to bond more with my children, help my daughter with her kindergarten syllabus, and help my son with his writing project. I personally wanted to clean, down-size, rest more, and finish my writing project.

6. Find the positive in everything. Spread that positivity to your children.

7. Teach children resilience by modeling your own strength. Smile. Remind each other that you will get through it.

8. Be gentle to yourself and kind to others.

9. Be gracious to everyone. Children are going to have questions, show certain behaviors, etc. Help them as much as you can.

10. Learn to live in the moment and enjoy the little things. My girls wanted to dress up, put on their new shoes, and play. I let them be. My son wanted to make origami and set traps and my younger daughter just wanted to snuggle with mommy. I just had to let them enjoy their moments. I enjoyed the touch of my children, their smiles, and their screaming and yelling and sibling squabbles as well. Our days are usually a rat race, but this time was quite relaxing in the midst of the fear of the virus and chaos.

END OF CHAPTER REFLECTIVE QUESTIONS

What is your experience as a family when you had to stay home, quarantine, and do school or work online during the coronavirus pandemic?

_____

_____

_____

How did you cope during the first few weeks and months of the pandemic when you first had to stay home, work, or support your children with virtual learning?

_____

_____

_____

What strategies and or routines did you have to learn, re-learn, unlearn, create and/or adjust to support yourself and your family during the pandemic?

_____

_____

_____

CHAPTER FIFTEEN: FOR THE DEPLOYED MILITARY PARENT

Hugs can do a great amount of good, especially for children.
—Princess Diana

IT WAS A WINTER SATURDAY morning in Japan, Yamaguchi prefecture to be precise. It was also the oyster festival season that particular weekend in that part of the country. I have a deep love for seafood, as does my whole family. We were on our way to the Oyster Festival in Miyajima, about an hour away from where we currently lived. We had to use the boat to cross to the island.

As the boat cruised its way across the sea to the next island, we decided to sit at the top of the deck to enjoy the scenery. It was cold but the sights and sounds were beautiful and entertaining. There were other boats, oyster farms in the water, and mountains in the distance. We could also feel the movement of the boat. Our children are curious, so they opted to stand and look down below. I was sitting close to them praying in my head that their curiosity did not drive any of them to try to jump into the water.

"What happens if I fall into the water, Daddy?" my son asked my husband. My heart raced and sank for a minute deeper in my stomach just hearing his question. "Daddy will jump into the water and rescue you, but do not jump into the water," my husband responded and warned. My son looked up at his dad and said, "Okay Daddy, I won't." I heaved a big sigh of relief hearing him say that. My children typically listen more to their father. Some people think it is because he is gone a lot and that they may be too used to be around me all the time. Whatever the psychology behind that is, I am not really sure.

He looked down at the water again and seemed to enjoy watching the waves dancing and the oyster farms all over in the water. My daughter also asked, "Is this the kind of ship you always go on Daddy?" He responded, "Not exactly." We had taken them to Norfolk in Virginia and Yokosuka in Japan to show them the big ships that my husband usually deploys with. Their question let me know that they could not remember those visits.

"You know, when Daddy is on the boat and I miss all of you and Mommy, I just come out to the deck and watch the water and the waves. It helps clear my mind sometimes," my husband explained to the children. They both stared back at him wanting to hear more. I wanted to hear more as well. We both share what we do occasionally to cope during deployments as we talk from time to time, but this conversation was getting interesting.

"Thank you for riding with us, and enjoy Miyajima," the guide announced, and we stepped out to be greeted, kissed, sniffed, and licked by the deer on the island that Saturday morning.

Deployments are hard for both the parent who must make the ship or another country his or her home several months in the year and the parent who feels left behind to figure it all out. It is even harder on the children.

I am writing this chapter not because I am the parent who has deployed, but the one who has stayed behind and witnessed children of different ages go through different things at home, school, daycare, and in the neighborhood or community. I have also spoken to several parents in uniform in writing this book to capture the stories that are often not publicly spoken about.

As the deployed parent, know that, most of all, your children will miss you. While you are gone, they may fall sick, they may develop habits (good and bad), and they may rebel or feel angry because you missed birthdays, school projects, and important events in their lives. Some may get used to you being gone all the time, and for some, it may take time. Some will admire you and will talk about how much you are a hero to them, and some may wonder why your work requires you to be gone for long periods of time.

In our family and in other military families that I have interacted with while writing this book, the deploying or deployed parent has found success with some of the following techniques to stay connected to their children, home, and family:

1. Write down important dates and make arrangements, if you can, before you leave for any deployment. Some servicemembers shared that writing down their children's birthdays, anniversary dates, and future graduation dates if they are going to miss it was helpful. They also mentioned that buying cards and small gifts and taking those with them so they could mail them back home to their children, spouses, and other family members did the trick. Mark mentioned that "there are not many options out there and sometimes nothing at all. More so, connectivity can be very slow when trying to buy something online, and I really want my family to know that I am thinking about them all the time."

2. Make arrangements and plans with other family members or friends who can order and deliver gifts in your absence, if possible. "In my last command, I used our ombudsman

to buy and deliver my wedding anniversary gift to my wife," said Brayden. "It was our tenth wedding anniversary, but I was not home. It worked out because the ombudsman was my wife's friend, and she knew the right colors to pick when I gave her an idea of what I wanted to get her."

3. Leave your family with a power of attorney and other key or important personal or proper documents.

4. Do not forget to update your Page 2. This is an important document to update, especially if there have been any major family changes, like marriage or new children.

5. Call and email your family often. Sometimes connectivity can be intermittent and emails and phone calls may not go through, but try to communicate when they work. My friend Ketrica, shared with me how her children are always looking forward to reading their Daddy's emails or hearing his voice over the phone, even if it is only for a few minutes.

6. Strive to create memories in the little time that you get to spend with your family before you embark on a deployment. For example, when you are home, spend time reading with and to the children, playing sports together, going to the park, playing boardgames, cooking, or even cleaning together. These memories are what will keep both you and your children together when you are all miles apart.

7. Go on deployment with things that connect you to your home and family. "I like to go with some artwork from my children and a few family photos," said Ryan, a military dad with two daughters. In my own case, my husband likes to bake with our oldest daughter, so I have seen him pack our small, homemade cookbook to take with him. "It reminds me of the wonderful times I get to spend with her when we are at home, and I look forward to coming home and baking with her," he said.

END OF CHAPTER REFLECTIVE QUESTIONS

Share your own experience planning for deployment with or without your family. What did you take with you?

_____

_____

_____

What other strategies have you used, or could you use to stay connected with your family when you are deployed or when you deploy next?

_____

_____

_____

What advice would you give as the active duty service member who must deploy to a brand new active duty member who is about to deploy for the first time leaving his family behind?

_____

_____

_____

CHAPTER SIXTEEN: GOING THROUGH TRAUMA AS A FAMILY

*If you do not take time to heal, you will bleed on the
people who never hurt you.*
—Unknown

SEPTEMBER 2018 WAS A VERY difficult time for us as a family. My children were seven, five, and three then. We had just moved into our beautiful home in Jacksonville, Florida in the spring and we thought it would be the happiest moment of our life. The year 2018 itself was a very confusing, overwhelming, and complicated transition and move for us as a military family. We had moved from Virginia Beach to Jacksonville but with follow-on overseas orders to Japan.

Since my husband had to report to our new squadron to start our next tour on a specific set date, he had taken the lead to Iwakuni, Japan while the children and I stayed behind and tried to figure out what our next plan was. In plain words, we needed to decide whether we were going to move and join him within the year or ask to modify the orders to *unaccompanied* so that the children and I did not have to move at all. My husband would serve two years overseas and return if we chose that route. It was a lot to think about and process and was a big decision for us. Fortunately, at the time, my own mom was still staying with us and helping us take care of our children as we navigated through this thought process.

We spent our first few months in Florida exploring the beautiful city and getting to know our neighbors. The weather in Florida is totally different from any other weather the children and I had experienced. The weather was nice. The sunshine kissed our bodies daily and we loved the smiles that everybody wore on their faces but living there every day was totally new and challenging in many other ways. One afternoon, for example, the rain poured non-stop, accompanied by strong winds and then a lightning strike, which hit our home directly. Yes, just our home. Our neighbors were just fine. It was the most traumatic weather experience I had ever had. In the midst of the thunderstorm, we heard a loud crash. My children screamed and started running all over around the house. Our lights went off, our TV went dead, and the sockets in the master bedroom cracked and sputtered. I stood there speechless and clueless. My children finally ran to find me downstairs and started asking me zillions of questions while screaming and crying at the same time because they were feeling scared. I tried to hold it all together and stand firm, but I saw myself slowing lowering my body down and sitting on the carpet as tears choked me. I felt the hands of my children around my shoulders. My mother followed, seeking answers that I did not have. I also heard my mom saying "awurade, awurade," in Twi, meaning *my God, my God.* I managed to look around as eight eyeballs look right back at me demanding answers. "Everything will be okay," I managed to say as I hugged each of my children but wanting everyone to just leave me alone to think. I needed to process what was happening and to find out what I needed to do in this new area where we really did not know many people. I also needed to find out who I could call and for what. The base was at least forty minutes away from our home. My husband was on a ship in the middle of nowhere in the ocean. Then I remembered that my friend Elisa was fifteen minutes away. I could call our builder, and even our next-door neighbors, who were kind enough to check in regularly on us once they learned my husband was serving overseas and deployed at the same time.

I also managed to check my phone and listened to the radio. We had a small radio that used batteries. I found the flashlight and lit some candles too. I saw on the internet and heard news of floods, homes being destroyed, and people being evacuated all around us. Family and friends called to find out if we were okay and let us know we could call them if we needed anything. They reassured us that they cared about us and that they were praying for us. I managed to get hold of the home insurance company. Luckily, we had non-perishable food and water for the next few days. I checked the car, and we had enough gas just in case we needed to evacuate. But we did not have to. Everything came back to normal after three days. I was grateful I had our emergency backpack stocked, which lasted the entire time we needed batteries, canned food, and the radio.

Just when we were recuperating from this weather event, we got a call from my home country, Ghana. When a phone call came from the village it was never good news because my Grandma still lived there and was sick. The call that came was not news about Grandma in the hospital but a shocking and devastating report that my uncle had passed away from food poisoning. Uncle Azong was my mother's younger and only brother from the same womb. He was strong, charming, and had a great sense of humor. When I lived with my Grandma, I spent time with him on the farm in the village. He would weed, sow, water the crops, and lead the harvest since both Grandma and Grandpa were pretty old. The news was a much bigger blow to my mom than any other person.

In the midst of grieving my uncle we had another call from the same village. This time it was my maternal grandma who had died. She had been sick and the news of my uncle passing away made things worse. "Grandma followed her son to the grave," my mom murmured in tears.

I saw my mother for the first time grieving for days and weeks. She wailed and talked and refused to eat or sleep.

On the other hand, I was so overwhelmed and traumatized that I could not feel a thing for a moment and for the few days that followed. I have fond memories of the only grandmother that I knew. This was the woman who had taken me in when I was barely four years old, bathed me, combed my hair every day, braided my hair most days, and walked me to school holding my hands and carrying my stool on her head. She cooked for me and still kept my toys—a red rubber doll and a small, shiny metal pot.

When I spoke to her the last time when my uncle had passed, she had this to say "Agifty, today that I have heard your voice, I will sleep well and my soul will be at peace." In my mother tongue Buli, a language spoken in Sandema (northern parts of Ghana), the letter A is added to many names when pronouncing it. So "Agifty" just meant *Gifty*, my name.

How was I going to explain to my children what I was going through at that moment?

Weather trauma.

Death trauma.

Deployment trauma.

Not to mention the drama of the children in all of this because they were upset that Daddy had been gone for such a long time. I had emailed my husband to let him know everything that had happened, though he was so far away from home. He called when he could, and he consoled and emailed as much as he could. My friend Elisa took us in for a couple of weeks to see if that can help us grieve and heal as a family. During this time, I cried, rested, and looked out for signs of trauma in my own children. I also researched and read about the subject and most importantly how best to support my own as well as other and children when the need arises.

SIGNS THAT CHILDREN ARE GOING THROUGH TRAUMA AND HOW YOU CAN SUPPORT THEM

The American Psychological Association (APA) describes trauma as an "emotional response to a terrible event like an accident, rape or natural disaster." This physical, emotional, real, or perceived events that cause traumatic experience in children and youth can be as a result of a single event or as a result from exposure to multiple events or situations over time. Some trauma types include natural disasters, bullying, community violence, death in the family, grief, physical abuse, and sexual abuse.

Trauma affects children's brains, behavior, emotions, and their physical bodies in different ways. Children will show different signs that can mean they might be experiencing some sort of trauma. Your child may look and feel overwhelmed or shocked or have difficulty processing the experience and even expressing themselves.

Emotionally, children who are experiencing trauma typically show feelings of low esteem, have difficulty bonding with caregivers, and have trouble making friends with peers and adults. Children may also go through various stages of emotions such as denial, anger, fear, sadness, shame, confusion, anxiety, depression, guilt, hopelessness, irritable, and difficulty in processing the events that led to the trauma.

Sometimes, children may show different behaviors. Parents and caregivers are usually confused and feel frustrated and helpless in understanding the underlying cause and what to do exactly. You can support your child who is experiencing trauma in different ways.

For example, it is always best to talk to your child and explain as much as you can. Also assure your child that whatever feelings they are going through are normal for anyone experiencing trauma and find what makes your child tick so you can use it to comfort, calm, and bring them back to composure. And finally, there always the military and family life consultants (MFLC) and FOCUS groups on the different bases who can offer a lot of support for you and the child. From my own experience, I have worked with MFLCs who visited our child and youth programs and worked with children and met with parents and offered trainings to support families.

END OF CHAPTER REFLECTIVE QUESTIONS

What do you know about trauma and what is your own experience with trauma with or without your children?

_____

_____

_____

Do you take notes of your own behavior and behaviors of your children from time to time during traumatic events?

_____

_____

_____

Do you know how and where to go for help for yourself or your family when you are going through trauma?

_____

_____

_____

CHAPTER SEVENTEEN: SUPPORTING CHILDREN WITH SPECIAL NEEDS

We have no special needs children, just children with special needs.
—Uwe Maurer

I AM GOING TO BE brutally honest with you here. The first time I encountered a child who needed extra care, love, patience, and support because they have special needs to be attended to, I had no clue what to do. I was starting out as a childcare professional at the time. Let me also admit that I was similar to most people at that time who would look stunned at a child and ask in my mind *but what is wrong with him?* There is nothing wrong with any child, in my opinion, but a whole lot can go wrong when adults fail to learn and adapt to how to care for and teach a child with special needs.

In my own scenario, growing up in Ghana and moving to the US later on in life, I had a whole ton of learning, relearning, unlearning, and adjusting to do in many ways. As far as children with special needs is concerned, I can say for sure that certain medical terminologies, diagnoses, and support for children with special needs was not popular when I was growing up. I believe the need existed, but they were just not named then. As a matter of fact, as a child we were allowed to scream when we needed to. We also roamed freely, played in the dirt, danced in the rain, licked the rainwater falling from the sky, and climbed trees, just to mention a few. My favorite tree to climb was the mango tree on my grandfather's friend's mango farm in Sandema Kori, in the Upper East region in Ghana. We were not labeled. It did not mean we were perfect children. I was not. My brother was not either. There were not too many four-walled classrooms, advanced and researched medical terminologies as is the case today. My mother and many other parents went on their knees first and prayed. They went to the church and ask for prayer support first before seeking medical help if they suspected we needed special attention that they could not wrap their head around or support. I hope you see the picture and that and that you catch the drift.

Hence, when I was thrown into an after school care program classroom at my very first job on US soil, I was in for a lot more shock than I anticipated. I had to tighten my belt and sit up straight in order to successfully work with all the wonderful children in my classroom. I was introduced to new concepts and strategies as far as children with special needs is concerned.

After a decade of working in the childcare profession, I have worked with children on different bases with special needs. I have also met parents raising children with special needs. Some of them are very close friends that I call family and we have coffee together sometimes.

I do not drink coffee, but on those days I do. I have also met other family members, including grandparents, who are supporting the raising of these children. I have worked and I still work with some of these children in different military child and youth programs on bases in the US and abroad. In addition, I work with other childcare professionals and early childhood education technicians who work to support these children.

So, what am I saying? From experience and with firsthand information from the horses own mouth, as a parent raising a child with special needs or a caregiver providing care for children with special needs, you are going to need all the knowledge, information, resources, and most importantly, the faith, courage, and hope. Let me emphasize that you are going to have to let go of guilt, shred your ego, and fight like a lion sometimes to get your children the resources they will need to succeed at home, school, daycare, and also to thrive in life. Most importantly, you will need to build a network of a supportive clan and learn to really take care of yourself so you can keep going on when you feel like giving up. And finally, you will find out that children with special needs are the ones who will inspire you to become a very special person for the world out there.

CATEGORIES OF CHILDREN WITH SPECIAL NEEDS

There are four major classifications of special needs. These are physical, developmental, behavior or emotional, and sensory impaired.

The physical needs category includes allergies, leukemia, chronic asthma, multiple sclerosis, muscular dystrophy, and epilepsy.

In my own experience, the first time I came into contact with a child with primarily physical need was a toddler named Kendall who had an extra finger on his left hand.

I remember stopping at the sink and staring hard at his fingers as I helped him wash his hands. Somehow, I wished I knew of the situation or all the facts earlier before I was thrown into the classroom to be his teacher. Kendall had the Jeune syndrome condition. Later, I researched and learned that Jeune syndrome is a rare condition that specifically affects the bones. Children born with Jeune syndrome usually have a small, narrow chest, short ribs, unusually shaped pelvis, shortened bones of the arm and legs, and also extra fingers and/or toes.

The second broad category of special needs is developmental, which includes autism, Down syndrome, dyslexia, and processing disorders. Children with autism may have problems thinking and behaving in a flexible way. They may scream or make funny noises. They tend to have trouble relating to the world around them or people around them. They want less noise and fewer people. Critically, they may have problems communicating clearly verbally or non-verbally.

The third category of special needs, behavioral needs, encompasses ADHD, eating disorders, bipolar disorder, and oppositional defiance disorder.

The fourth is sensory impairment, such as being blind, visually impaired, learning impaired, or deaf.

Children with special needs typically exhibit different behaviors and signs. The type of the special need and support available will largely depend on the diagnosis.

It is very important to know that every child has specific needs, skills, and wants. In other words, all children with special needs manifest, learn, cope, and experience differently.

LEGAL PROTECTIONS FOR CHILDREN WITH SPECIAL NEEDS

In the US, there are state and federal laws that protect all children with special needs. The first legal protection of note is the Individuals with Disabilities Education Act (IDEA), which stipulates that students with disabilities must be prepared for further education, employment, and independent living.

The second legal protection is seen in the Rehabilitation Act, which prohibits schools from discriminating against children with disabilities and requires schools to provide accommodations for disabled children.

The Americans With Disabilities Act (ADA) specifies that schools must meet the needs of children with psychiatric problems.

Finally, No Child Left Behind requires schools to uphold the achievement standards for children with disabilities.

STRATEGIES TO SUPPORT CHILDREN WITH SPECIAL NEEDS AT HOME AND IN A DAYCARE OR SCHOOL SETTING

The popular quote that *If a child cannot learn the way we teach, maybe we should teach the way they learn* is a necessary reminder to fully include and support children in their upbringing and learning. As the parent, caretaker, guardian, or caregiver you'll want to take time and effort to:

- Learn as much as you can
- Stay informed with the latest information and policies
- Help children express their needs and wants
- Help your children express their anxieties
- Create and follow simple routines
- Do activities together
- Introduce small or new things one at a time
- Manage expectations
- Adjust routines when needed

TIPS FOR CARING FOR THE CAREGIVER

Caring for children with special needs can be exhausting. It can leave you empty and make you feel like you are a failure. My friend Majia shares with me how she is constantly tired, exhausted, and feeling sleepy a lot of days as a result of constantly have to care and support her child with special needs.

Families with special needs usually go through stages when the diagnosis is announced. They go through denial, depression, and rage. Allowing yourself to go through the process is key. In addition to that, identifying peak moments that are highly stressful is helpful as you seek help and support for yourself. Connecting with other parents raising children with special needs will help you because sharing ideas and having the listening ear of someone who truly understands what you are feeling really makes a difference. And don't forget to ask for help so you can get rest or sleep from trusted family and friends.

END OF CHAPTER REFLECTIVE QUESTIONS

What does supporting children with special needs mean to you?

_____

_____

_____

What would you change about the way military children with special needs receive the services they need if you have the power?

_____

_____

_____

In what one way can you support a family you know who is raising a child with special needs?

_____

_____

_____

CHAPTER 18: BEFORE YOU GO, LET'S HAVE A HEART-TO-HEART TALK

To a child, "love" is spelled "T.I.M.E."
—Zig Ziglar

A GOOD NUMBER OF DAYS, you are going to think and feel like you don't know what you are doing as a parent. You are not alone. Most parents I know, including myself, have days and times where we question what and how we are doing as far as raising our children is concerned. This is why *Growing Your Family* is an invitation to travel along with me on the journey of learning how to nurture children with parents in uniform. Our military children.

I did not only invite you but gave you a glimpse into my own life as a military spouse and mom and have shown you some of our life as a military family. I have also poured out my heart and shared without shame my own lived experience as a military spouse and mom on how we are grinding along yet grounding well as a family. You have indeed been challenged to take steps to flourish and given ideas that can help you thrive as a military family given the uniqueness of the military career field and family lifestyle. What we have signed up for as military families is in no way a piece of cake or a bowl of *miso soup* but a life extraordinaire that calls for making intentional efforts and taking micro steps in order to thrive and flourish. It is worth every sweat.

Since I made a silent promise to all military children, (especially the ones I work with and my own) to have a tête-à-tête with parents, I cannot conclude this book without mentioning a few more important things:

Do not be too busy for your child. Life is real in the military home. It can be messy, chaotic, busy, and crazy fun with everything thrown at the family sometimes with or without prior short notice. Between Permanent Change of Duty Station (PCS) moves, deployments, and caring for children it is easy to be consumed by the busyness of the military lifestyle. Be brutal about creating and protecting some time just for you and your child, even if it is for just a few moments in the midst of the craziness. This may mean saying *no* to some people and not participating in every event or being the one to solve all the problems for everyone you know. This also means putting in effort and dedicating about fifteen to twenty minutes to read a bedtime story to your child, taking your child to the park for about thirty minutes, and making time to play a game with your child at home. Children remember these moments and the memories that you are creating together.

Listen to your child talk all the time. Let's just face it. Sometimes your children will talk your ear to death. Several times when we are driving home after a hard day's work, I just feel like jumping out of the car when my children start talking non-stop, accompanied by whining, crying, squabbling, or even laughing aloud. My work requires me to facilitate training workshops and coaching childcare staff for the most part of the day, so at the end of the day I am just done talking or listening to anybody or anything. To help me become a better listener or in a better position to respond to my children as we drive home after a hard day's grind, I make time to go for short walks, take short breaks, and also hit the gym even if it's only for thirty minutes before my shift ends. Sometimes, just simply breathing in and out and reminding myself that I am a mom puts me in a better situation to listen to my children on our drive home. Other times, I just ask open-ended questions like "which part of today did you enjoy most at school?" and direct the talk from whining and squabbling to really sharing their highs and lows about their day, the new student, or cool project.

Hug your child often. Be the last one to break the hug. Physical touch is key to children's emotional health and development. A caring hug from someone they love makes them feel secured, cared for, loved, comforted, and helps build their self-esteem. Make the effort to hug your children often throughout the day—before bedtime, before you drop them off at school or daycare, and when you pick them up. Also hug your child for no special reason or occasion at all. When you hug them tight, do not be in a hurry to let go of the hug, let them be the one to break the hug. Children can sense that you do not have time for them when you just want to rush out by breaking the hug fast. This could mean to your children that they do not matter. Oftentimes, we have had to explain to our children that a brief hug does not mean we do not love them and that sometimes Daddy or Mommy just have to go catch a plane or be on time to an appointment.

Do not substitute your presence for presents. Simply put, do not bribe your children with presents or gifts instead of making time for them. It is different when the deployed parent wants to send home thoughtful presents. When you are not deployed or traveling for work, making time to play with your children is more important than finding excuses to avoid them and then buying them expensive gifts to compensate for not being present.

Love your child hard. Show them you love them. Children grow fast and pick up on a lot of things. Sometimes children's interpretation of what you do or fail to do can be tricky. Show your children you love them by doing different things. For example, play with your child, color together, sing together, dance together, blow bubbles together, play sports together, ride together, bake together, cook simple recipes together, and, last but not the least, laugh much and often together.

END OF CHAPTER REFLECTIVE QUESTIONS

Describe how you strive to connect and spend time together as a family. What do you do exactly?

_____

_____

_____

What specific ideas would you like to share with other military families on how you SHOW your children you LOVE them?

_____

_____

_____

Share what you are doing or would do differently to help you and your family flourish and thrive?

_____

_____

_____

RESOURCES TO HELP YOUR CHILD

GENERAL PARENTING INFORMATION AND RESOURCES

www.infoaboutkids.org
This organization provides parents with science-based information on parenting topics related to the emotions, minds, and bodies of children as a way of promoting healthy children and family development.

www.militaryonesource
This resource provides valuable information and programs for military parents.

www.childwelfare.gov
This resource has valuable information that helps strengthen families and protect children.

www.militarychildcare.com
This website provides information and helps parents find care, whether center-based or home care on military installations.

https://4-hmilitarypartnerships.org

This organization focuses on positive youth development in communities.

https://www.choosemyplate.gov/

My Plate helps children learn healthy eating habits. The also have easy recipes that you can cook with your children.

EDUCATIONAL SERVICES AND PROGRAMS

https://military.tutor.com

Tutor.com is funded by the Department of Defense and Coast Guard Mutual Assistance and offers free online tutoring as well as homework help to military children.

https://abcmouse.com

ABCmouse.com is an early learning platform for children that is designed to help children as early as pre-school.

https://www.ourmilitarykids.org

Our military kids is an entity that strongly believes that children whose parents are in the military serve too and aims at supporting military family resiliency through funding sports activities, arts, and other enrichment programs.

https://www.coolmath.com/

This resource has math games, lessons, and practice sheets for children.

RESOURCES TO HELP CHILDREN BOOST THEIR CONFIDENCE

http://biglifejournal.com
Big Life Journal has printouts and books to keep children busy learning by completing self-love and self-confidence challenges and activities.

https://focusproject.org/
The FOCUS (Families Overcoming Under Stress) project offers resilience training for military children, families, and couples. Participants learn necessary skills, such as communication, emotional regulation, problem solving, goal setting, and managing trauma.

RESOURCES FOR CHILDREN WITH SPECIAL NEEDS

Exceptional Family Member Program (EFMP)
This program is available to all military children and family members who have physical, emotional, intellectual, or developmental disorders and require specialized services.

Educational and Developmental Intervention Services (EDIS)
This program supports families of children with developmental delays, disabilities, or special learning needs.

http://www.p2pusa.org
Parent to Parent USA provides help for parents of children with special needs.

http://www.frcd.org

This organization supports parents of children with special needs with assistance, training, and information to help the whole family.

https://www.autism-society.org/

The Autism Society provides information for individuals on the autistic spectrum, family members, and professionals.

http://cec.sped.org

The Council for Exceptional Children offers resources and information about special education.

http://www.napcse.org/

The National Association of Parents with Children in Special Education (NAPCSE) is a national membership organization that offers assistance to parents whose children receive special education services in or out of school.

http://www.familyvoices.org/

Family Voices is a network of family and friends of children and youth with special healthcare needs and disabilities.

http://fcsn.org/

The Federation for Children with special needs aims at providing resources and support for parents with children with special needs.

RESOURCES ON SCHOLARSHIPS AND GRANTS FOR MILITARY CHILDREN

There are various national and local scholarships and grants for military children and families. Each scholarship opportunity has its own requirements, application deadlines, and unique package. The best way is to identify scholarship opportunities and start applying early. The various installations have representatives who can walk you through available grants options as well. Here are a few scholarships and grants to explore.

https://amvets.org/scholarships/
The American Veterans (AMVETS) scholarship is for children and families of honorably discharged veterans, Active Duty, Guards and Reserves who are high school seniors.

https://daughters1894.org/scholarship/
Daughters of The Cincinnati scholarship is available to daughters of career commissioned officers of the United States Armed Services.

http://www.militarychildoftheyear.org/
This award goes to a military child each year who invents a bold and creative solution that addresses a local, reginal, or global challenge.

https://ncoausa.org/benevolent-programs/scholarship-fund/
The Non Commissioned Officers Association (NCOA) scholarship fund has the sole purpose of assisting dependents of NCOA members pursue higher education.

https://militaryscholar.org/sfmc/
Scholarships for Military Children is a scholarship program that aims at supporting the educational goals of military families through the Fisher House Foundation.

https://militarywithkids.com/100-military-kids-scholarships/
This website helps with the navigation of branch specific scholarships and other scholarships.

ACKNOWLEDGMENTS

I COULD NOT HAVE PULLED this project off without the enormous support, timely guidance, and authentic personal stories of all the wonderful people I have met on this writing journey and in my life. As an avid listener, I am grateful for the individuals who have poured out their pure stories, deep knowledge, and raw experiences of parenting military children. Your stories touched me and shaped my perspective as I grappled with my own parenting questions along the way being a Christian immigrant mom, a military spouse, and a professional who works with children in military childcare programs. The result is this beautiful work. Some names in this book have been changed to protect the privacy of the individuals I interacted with and whose stories I have compiled with their permission and shared in this book.

A huge thank you to my village of parents who have genuinely and openly shared a part of their lives with me. I am truly grateful. You are my heroes and sheroes. I have been moved by your courage, your resilience, and above all, your kindness.

I am highly indebted to my dream partners for this project. For those who willingly read some pages and asked thought-provoking questions to help me craft this in a better way to serve my readers.

I offer special thanks to my team of professionals who helped me put this book together, notably my editorial team, designers and publishers at Koehler Books.

My mother, Mama Lydia, deserves my biggest thank you. *Maman* you gave life to me and raised me to believe in myself. You have taught me to chart my own life course without permission, including releasing this book.

Thank you to my younger brother Lawson. You gave me a chance to be your parent when I was still a child myself. Thank you for believing in me and trusting the process along the way.

A very big thank you goes to my big brother Joe and dear sisters from the other womb—Comfort, Janet (Mama Cheri), Elizabeth (Mama Lizzy), Margaret (Mama TT), Grace, and Yvonne. I have seen each of you raise your children with relentless sacrifice. You all modeled resilience, love, and unity. Thank you for contributing to my own growth.

Most importantly, to all the wonderful people God placed in my life growing up whom I could not mention in this book, but you know yourselves. You were there for me as my parents, brothers, sisters, and friends. You are indeed proof that family can be formed outside the bloodline.

And finally, to my family, especially my husband and children. A huge thanks to my husband and friend Maxwell for your unconditional love and for being an epitome of patience, kindness, and peace in our home. Thank you for making this dream come true.

For my children, Max Jr, Meghan, and Maya. Thank you for your patience and enthusiasm on this journey:

Max Jr. for being gentle, caring, and the best big brother ever to your little sisters, which helped me learn more about you on this journey.

Meghan, our daring fire. You bring love and laughter to our home with your personality. You danced and twirled, putting a smile on my face as I wrote this book. Thank you.

Maya, our boss lady but also our calming water. Your quiet demeanor brings peace and tranquility to our home. You remind us that sometimes what is not planned is the best that can happen to us. Thank you for snuggling peacefully on the couch with me as I wrote this book.

To you all my children, I am proud to say that you are all the inspiration behind this book. I have always said that, if nothing at all, I am writing this book for you. I want my daughters and son to hold in their hands what they challenge me to do and the blessing in doing it every day as their mother. You are truly a blessing to me, and this is for you in return.

And above all, I would like to thank God Almighty for his grace, wisdom, and strength for it all.

ABOUT THE AUTHOR

PEARL ALIMO, AKA GIFTY, is married to her high school sweetheart Maxwell Alimo, a sailor who has been serving the United States Navy since 2008. Together, they have three wonderful children. They have served in different commands and lived on different bases throughout the United States and in Japan.

Pearl is not only a military spouse and a mother of three, but also a career woman and an advocate for girl's education. She is the Founder of the Greight Foundation, a project that is dedicated to mentoring girls from harsh backgrounds to pursue their education and career goals in life.

Her deep love for children and youth led her to pursue a career in childcare. Since 2011, she has worked with the different branches of the military child and youth programs and is currently a training and curriculum specialist. In her work, she finds joy and purpose in training childcare professionals to run quality child and youth programs that serve military children from different cultural backgrounds and family dynamics. She sees this as her way of supporting the US military to be mission ready.

The most fulfilling part of her work outside growing her own family is growing other people. Pearl heads Greight Company, LLC—a career consulting firm that offers career support services and programs to individuals, teams and agencies where she mainly trains, coaches, and supports others to succeed in their careers.

Pearl Alimo holds a bachelor's degree in French and linguistics from the University of Ghana-Legon and a master's degree in education from Michigan State University. She enjoys reading writing, traveling with her family, and eating sushi. You can connect with Pearl at https://www.pearlgalimo.com, on Facebook at https://www.facebook.com/pearlgalimo and on Instangram as pearlg.alimo.